Our Morocco

Moroccans and Expats Share Their
Lives, Hopes, Dreams, and Adventures

© Journey Beyond Travel Publications

All rights reserved. This book or any portion thereof may not be reproduced or used in any manner whatsoever without the express written permission of the publisher except for the use of brief quotations in a book review. All works are the rights of their authors. Images are copyrighted by the authors and/or photographers and/or creators wherever they appear. All opinions are the opinions of their creators and do not necessarily reflect the opinions of Journey Beyond Travel. Then again, if you are reading this, you likely already knew that. This is just a reminder in case you did not. Did you like our cover? We sure do! We begged and pleaded and finally Dina gave in and created this glorious, fun, happy, pop-a-licious cover that gives a great big hug to all of the wonderful stories within. We sincerely hope you this adds a bit of happiness to your bookshelf or maybe even better your nightstand. All the proceeds of this anthology will go to a really wonderful foundation that helps to build libraries in some of the furthest reaches of Morocco. You'll read lots more about this foundation soon. Suffice to say, it is incredible and your support is truly appreciated. You really do make a difference. Journey Beyond Travel Publications is a division of Journey Beyond Travel, Morocco's premier in-country tour operator. JOURNEY BEYOND TRAVEL name and LOGO are trademarked and copyrighted in the US and abroad. COVER DESIGN: Dina Benbrahim. BOOK LAYOUT & DESIGN: Siraj Abbad. EXTRA DESIGN AID: Alison Bailey. FOR OLIVE SEED & THE MOROCCO LIBRARY PROJECT: Barb Mackraz. COPY EDITOR: Zora O'Neall. EDITOR: Lucas Peters.

First Edition

14 13 12 11 10 / 10 9 8 7 6 5 4 3 2 1

ISBN 9798575846093

Journey Beyond Travel Publications
8 rue Senhaja, Suite 61
Tangier 90000
MOROCCO

www.journeybeyondtravel.com

All proceeds from the sale of this anthology support literacy in Morocco through the Morocco Library Project by Olive Seed.

Thank you for your contribution!

For more information on the Morocco Library Project, please visit:
https://www.moroccolibraries.org

For more information about Olive Seed, please visit:
https://www.oliveseed.org

Discover more about Morocco on our award-winning blog:
https://www.journeybeyondtravel.com/blog

Table of Contents

Foreword 13
   by Barb Mackraz

Letter from the Editor 17
   by Lucas Peters

Fez Under Lockdown 21
   text and photos by Suzanna Clarke

Coming to Grips with Morocco: The Three Stages ... 33
   by Eirlys Davies

Headfirst into the Hammam 45
   by Amanda Mouttaki

Rootless Plant 51
   by Hazim Azghari

The Making of a Saint 61
> by Lucas Peters

A Memoir of Home 71
> by Zakariaa Aitouraies

Nothing Is Certain 77
> by Richard Hamilton

My Country(wo)men & Artisans 85
> text and photos by Amina Lahbabi

Gratitude from the Windy City of Essaouira 97
> by Lynn Houmdi

A Biased Typographical Collection of Tangier 109
> by Dina Benbrahim

A Night with the Nomads 121
> by Alice Morrison

Tales Told to a Melon 127
> by Tahir Shah

Living in a Museum in Tangier 145
> by Gerald Loftus

Couscous Friday 153
> by Myronn Hardy

Top Ten Reasons I Love Morocco …Roughly in the order I encountered them 161
> by Zora O'Neill

Morocco Is 171
> by Saeida Rouass

About the Authors 177

Foreword

by Barb Mackraz
Founder & Director of the Morocco Library Project

Before you read any further, I need to say thank you. The book you hold in your hands will help bring more libraries and literacy programs to young people in rural Morocco. With generosity of the writers and artists you'll discover in these pages, as well as a big assist from the team at Journey Beyond Travel, we have ensured that all proceeds of this anthology will go to fund the Morocco Library Project. Let me tell you a little more about what exactly the Morocco Library Project is and how it came to be.

The Morocco Library Project (or "MLP" as the kids like to call it) started simply with one little library in the town of Erfoud, near the Algerian border, right at the edge of the Sahara Desert.

When I first visited Morocco in 2013, I had no plan of visiting the desert, let alone build a library. I had planned on going to see the arts of the imperial cities, seeking the beautiful geometry of Islamic art and architecture, but then our guide, an Amazigh named Muha, talked us into crossing the Atlas Mountains to see the other side of his country. When our car began its long descent down the mountain and into the Sahara, I couldn't help it. I was captivated.

Muha had arranged for met to meet with local high school students. I sat at a round table with twenty teenagers chatting with me. Over the course of our conversation, each one of them had told me the name of book they dreamed of reading, even though there was "no place called library" in the region and no real opportunity for young people to develop a culture of reading. My first thought was honest amazement. "These kids are on the edge of a great leap forward." This thought stuck in my mind.

My second thought was more concrete and, if I'm being honest, forced me into action.

"Why don't we build them a library? After all, how hard could it be?"

To make a long story short, when I got back home to California, I set to work immediately to take this thought out from my head and make it a reality. It seemed like such a simple, if slightly crazy, idea — and I had no idea what it would set in motion.

For that first library, those same twenty students fixed up an old room in their school and painted some of the walls purple, my favorite color. This first library became wildly successful and quickly became known throughout the country.

The next thing I knew, teachers from all over Morocco were writing me asking for a library of their own. I still had a day job. I was working in Silicon Valley in the tech field. But building libraries? Amassing knowledge? This wasn't a job, it was an honest calling. I couldn't have my day job and be able to build libraries halfway across the planet. So, I did the only thing I could imagine myself doing — I quit my career to pursue this labor of love.

This was when the MLP really took off as a program. We decided to build the second library. A student had written me to say that her teacher, Abdelhaq, had "built bookshelves in hopes of having books one day." Who can resist that plea? Another decision was made. Another library built. Like that, we were well on our way.

MLP partners directly with people, and that is why it works. The goal is simply to help teachers develop a love of learning and a culture of reading, by providing students access to enjoyable books, a treasure they have never had. Those of us who grew up with books and libraries are the fortunate ones, and the MLP is all about sharing that bounty. This also builds good global citizens. When a student named Fatima Zahra writes us to say she is the first woman in her family to go to college, and it's thanks to the library, that's a success that will have a positive ripple effect as she becomes a role model to other young women in the future. And as long as teachers like Ali tell us that MLP has "sparked the candles" of his students, we will keep doing what we're doing.

MLP is a collaboration with teachers. We work with after-school English clubs, where the teachers have the freedom to develop creative activities beyond the test-based curriculum of the regular school day. Most of the students involved are going on to university, the first in their families, and many are the children of nomads or former nomads. Imagine the transformation that can take place in one generation! This has an outsized impact on girls, who join the English clubs in great numbers once they have a library. Girls in our communities in Morocco love to read. An after-school club with a library provides a welcome space for them.

The beauty of a library like ours is seeing young people blossom. One student, Ferdawss, read fifty books in a year. Ever since she has written book reviews of young adult novels. We share her reviews with others across the network to inspire other young people to pick up a book. Another student, Kawtar, was so captivated by a biography of Rachel Carson that she started an environmental club and planted trees. Mohcine became an environmental activist in Morocco after reading about the loss of biodiversity. Fatima-Zahra wrote that because of MLP, "I am alive."

Now, seven years later, MLP is all over the country. We are concentrated particularly in Amazigh communities in the South and the Southeast. There are now just over thirty libraries, some large, some small, and each one a platform for a lot of good things to happen.

I hope you'll enjoy this modest treasure chest of stories. I am truly grateful for everyone who has been a part of this. So, on behalf of the teachers and the kids who frequent the libraries around Morocco that we've been fortunate enough to build, I also cannot thank you, the reader, enough for your support!

If you'd like to know more about MLP and other ways you can be involved, please visit us at: https://www.moroccolibraries.org.

Till then, *yallah*! Pour yourself a cup of sweet mint tea, imagine the scent of Essaouira orange blossoms in the air, and read on!

Letter from the Editor

by Lucas Peters

Dear Reader,

I've been stuck with a mean case of writer's block for a few weeks now. Every time I pick up the pen, sit at a typewriter, or start plugging away on my laptop to write this letter, nothing has seemed to spark the exact note I want you to hear. However, today of all days, the note sprang to my ears. I woke in the calm dark of the early morning to the pitter-patter of rain. It pittered off the hulking oleander tree just outside of the bedroom window and then pattered onto the patio below. An early winter symphony; a prelude of those cozy winter months to come. Visions of fireside book reading and family Scrabble nights danced through my imagination. It was in this moment that I realized the exact note I wanted you to hear and that note is *gratitude*. Who knew that gratitude sounded so much like the drizzling rain of the first winter storm?

So, while I am basking in this gratitude for you and for this anthology you hold in your hand, let me tell you about how *Our Morocco* came about.

Back in May 2020, as the world was reeling from the pandemic, I sat with my son in our office. We were working on his reading skills. He was just four years old and, in the next room, his newborn sister was sound asleep. I was grateful in that moment (and many moments before and since) to be able to teach my child to read. Many children, particularly in Morocco and other countries around Africa, do not have that basic opportunity — an opportunity which many of us from other parts of the world do.

Reading. It truly is fundamental.

While my son was in my arms, a well-loved copy of *The Cat in the Hat* opened on my lap, I had a flash of insight that quickly became this anthology. *What if I could ask some of the writers and artists I knew around Morocco to contribute a piece for an anthology? What if we could have the proceeds of this anthology go to a great cause?*

I fired off a quick email to a handful of writers. I knew that if they agreed, we could make something happen.

The responses piled into my inbox more quickly than I could respond. I was, and remain, amazed and humbled by the willingness of everyone included in these pages to spend their time in the midst of this pandemic writing for this anthology and, by extension, supporting the Morocco Library Project. Not only have they opened doors into their own private experience of my adopted country, but they worked countless hours putting up with my editorial demands, long phone calls at all hours of the day and night, and horrendously long-winded emails. Once more, they have done this all free-of-charge, just because, like me, they believe reading is fundamental and should be made accessible to everyone.

In these pages, you will travel all over Morocco. No doubt, you will find some familiar names and revisit some familiar places. I must admit I found a special sort of comfort nestling back into the Jinn-haunted digs of Tahir Shah's Dar Khalifa in Casablanca. It was hard not to enjoy camping out again with the semi-nomadic friends of Alice Morrison and dipping a spoon into the traditional Friday afternoon couscous with Myronn Hardy in the quiet folds of the Middle Atlas. As always, I remain as linguistically confused from Fez to Tangier as Zora O'Neall. Perhaps more than any writer, I feel a true bond with Richard Hamilton as we both remain just as entranced as we often are befuddled while attempting to peel back the folds of Moroccan history. Of course vividly remembering that first awkward hammam experience with Amanda Mouttaki was a sheer delight, as was the enchantment I felt at Saeida Rouass's poetic ode to her very intimate Morocco. Meanwhile, Suzanna Clarke's insight as to how her community in Fez has responded to the pandemic is nothing short of inspirational, particularly in these difficult days.

In addition to some of these people you might well know, it is my sincere hope that you'll also meet a few new friends along the way. With Lynn Houmdi and Eirlys Davies, I couldn't help but think of my first few years in Morocco and all the necessary adjustment — physical, emotional, and mental — that this entailed. Hazim Azghari and Gerald Loftus have been so kind to open doors to their own private Moroccos, each a wonderful introspection that speaks to a very individual experience that very few of us will likely have the joy of repeating. Dina Benbrahim takes us on a bouncy typographic tour of Tangier as only she could, while Zakariaa Aitouraies brings us in on his reflection about what being Moroccan means to him. And of course, though I am well acquainted with the photography of Amina Lahbabi (she is my über-talented wife after all), I am sure you will enjoy her photographic contributions that grace these pages and give you a glimpse into the Morocco that captures her eye.

Of all the things that have gone into creating this anthology, I'm perhaps most proud of the fact that we have managed to include a number of Moroccan voices — voices that are typically glossed over, ignored, or shuffled to the margins. I hope that their voices give balance to this work. If I've done my job correctly, these pages should reflect the immense diversity of the country which inspired them. Immigrants and expats, Moroccans and foreigners alike — it truly is "our" Morocco.

An additional huge thank you is necessary for Dina Benbrahim for not only her words, but for designing this gorgeous cover. There is another gargantuan *shokran* in order for Zora O'Neall for her superhuman copywriting efforts. The whole of this anthology would be a lot messier if it were not for her eagle eye. I promise you, any mistakes you find in these pages are my fault, not hers.

It is my sincere hope that you be inspired by the stories found here and, insh'Allah, find your way to Morocco, whether for the first time or to revisit a good friend.

Literally 100% of all proceeds of this anthology go to support building libraries, sourcing books, and paying staff in the rural regions of Morocco. That is truly awesome.

Gratitude. I am filled with it because of you.

Gratefully Yours,

Lucas Peters, Managing Director
Journey Beyond Travel
Dar Kharoubia, Tangier
26 November, Thanksgiving Day, 2020

Fez Under Lockdown
text and photos by Suzanna Clarke

Lockdown in Morocco arrived with the force of a tsunami. At the beginning of 2020, I had watched, with detachment, news about far-flung places grappling to deal with a new kind of virus. Wrapped in the reassuring familiarity of my life in the Fez medina, such a problem seemed potentially inconvenient, but far from devastating.

In early March, our nearest European neighbors — Spain, France, and Italy — were swamped by the rapidly advancing wave of COVID-19 cases. My new assistant, having gone on a two-day trip to Spain to renew her Moroccan visa, found herself locked out of the country when the Spanish border closed without warning. I had been less than prescient with my advice.

I said, "I am sure it will be fine. They won't just close the border today."

On March 19, a state of emergency was declared, and that is exactly what they did. Not only did they close all land and air borders in Morocco, but it was announced that the border would also be closing for the indefinite future.

I made multiple calls to track down a group of Australians wandering around the Sahara, out of mobile range. They were finally contacted, and they managed to make a mad dash to Marrakesh airport. They queued for days to get the seats on the last flights in a scene reminiscent of the fall of Saigon.

As the Fez medina emptied of its conga lines of tourists, and anyone else who had another place to be departed, an uneasy calm descended.

*   *   *

Following the swift border closure, a quarantine was announced. We would begin lockdown on March 25, with some of the strictest regulations in the world. To leave the house, we would need permission from the local authorities, and only one member of a household would be able to leave at a time, and then only for necessities. Grocery stores and pharmacies were to remain open, but everything else — restaurants, cafés, mosques, and businesses deemed non-essential — were to shutter.

The night before the lockdown began, locals stood on their rooftops with candles, chanting and praying for Allah's protection. This seemed to be an entirely sensible response, given the unknown nature of what we were facing.

The following night, my family and I heard shouting and loud noises from afar, and wondered what was going on. It turned out that there were protests in the city, by a group who opposed closing the mosques, shops, and businesses.

However, the government was resolute. It had decided that a strict lockdown, before there were many active cases, was an immediate necessity. For that, my husband, Sandy, and I were relieved. As we had watched the leaders of other countries dither and be overcome by the rapid rise in cases, we were glad to be living in a country with a government that could make such a unilateral decision, and implement it so quickly.

Not much work for cleaners on the quiet Ta'laa Sghira

Masks were, as yet, a rarity, so it was necessary to improvise. I wrapped a scarf around my face and donned bright pink rubber gloves, resembling a cleaning lady turned bank robber.

Chasing down the local city council member who signed the movement permits for our area — necessary to step outside the house — took the better part of two days. I eventually cornered him on the street and, in my dodgy Arabic, persuaded him to sign; the effect of my winning smile was somewhat muted by the new face-scarf arrangement.

Roadblocks had appeared in multiple parts of the city. They were manned by tall young policemen wearing surgical masks. They took a keen interest in viewing permits and turned back those without legitimate business.

In some parts of the city, soldiers and their all-terrain vehicles were stationed at roadblocks, reinforcing the sense of a country under siege.

My guesthouse, Dar Malika, and the Medina Children's Library, which I helped to run, were forced to close, and the edges of my world shrank considerably. While I had a great affection for the riad where I had lived for the past decade, staying home was simultaneously pleasurable and claustrophobic.

* * *

The days developed a familiar pattern, quickly blending into one another.

Sandy and I rose early. We sipped coffee and crunched toast while reading the papers online. The coo of pigeons and the cheeping of sparrows broke the morning silence. We relished this period of peace, before little feet descended the stairs, and one or both of our small children appeared, wanting cuddles and breakfast. Aged five and three, Zaki and Malika relished this strange new state of affairs, in which their parents were permanently on call.

Mornings were filled with fitness sessions, homeschooling, drawing, and making things. The kids usually spent the afternoon playing in the fountain. I would escape for a couple of hours to my first-floor study, to catch up on work or have a siesta, before descending to make dinner.

My study is in the massariya. In earlier centuries it had been an apartment for the oldest son or honored guests. It consists of two adjoining rooms, overlooking the blue-and-white-tiled courtyard. The branches of an orange tree rustle against one of the windows, and, when ripe, fruit frequently falls, exploding in a sticky mess on the tiles below.

Surrounding the interior of the massariya are stained-glass windows with flower patterns, framed by intricately carved plaster. The date in the plaster reads 1292 in Islamic years. In the Gregorian calendar that is 1875. It is not the age of the riad, which is at least two centuries older, but when the plaster and the windows were installed.

The ceiling is the treasure of the house. It is cedar wood, carved and painted in a geometric pattern that radiates outwards. Sometimes I lay on the floor and stared up, imagining myself traveling to distant galaxies.

*   *   *

After two weeks of lockdown, I left the house for the first time. It felt surreal to walk the streets and alleys. Gone were the cafés full of men, where news was exchanged, transactions done, sports watched. Gone were the schoolchildren eating a hurried breakfast while walking to class. Gone were the housewives stopping to chat on their way to the hammam or the souk. Gone were the youths hanging around on street corners and the donkeys carrying building supplies or rubbish.

In the life before lockdown, I would hurry along, exchanging greetings as I went. I would call a cheery "Salaam alykum" to the owner of the local ḥanoot , a plump, worried-looking man who worked long hours at his little hole-in-the-wall shop. I would give a few coins to the blind beggar, with his milky eyes, black beard, and staff, who sat at the confluence of two streets, and then wave to the round-faced woman with her child who sat in the entrance of a chicken shop every day, no matter the weather.

Tribute to the King and Covid workers near R'Cif

Now the shops and workshops were shuttered and the streets devoid of human life. It was as though aliens had done a mass abduction of humans, leaving only the buildings and the odd cat.

This was far from the first time the Fez medina had experienced a plague. Over the centuries, the residents had been in lockdown many times.

In 1348, the Black Plague, emanating from Europe by way of the Far East, had a severe impact on Morocco. Then in 1595, the Saadian Empire collapsed because of another plague brought by Moriscos, Sephardic Jews and Andalusian Moors escaping the fall of Spain. A refugee camp was established just outside the walls, at the top of the medina, and conditions were far from sanitary. At its height, more than one thousand people in Fez died in a single day. Although the plague spread throughout Morocco, the region surrounding Fez was the most affected.

Between 1599 and 1601, the plague retreated. However, there was a fresh outbreak in 1607, which saw between a third and a half of the Moroccan population of seven million perish.

The eighteenth and nineteenth centuries were particularly grim. In 1799, the city of Fez was locked down for an entire year, and deaths from plague were up to 2,500 per day. The decades that followed brought six cholera epidemics and five famines.

Things didn't improve a great deal in the twentieth century, with episodes of typhus, malaria, plague, and smallpox each taking their turn between 1911 and 1944, to cause suffering to the people of the region. Not to forget the Spanish flu, which arrived at the end of 1918 and depopulated entire villages in the Rif Mountains.

Epidemics where there were a large number of deaths had the perverse effect of making the society more prosperous. When people died, their houses and possessions were passed on to their surviving relatives or, if they had none, to the religious authority. In this way, wealth was redistributed.

In more recent years, with a public health regimen and mass vaccinations, such illnesses became rare events. I had lived in the Medina for more than a decade and never seen a major outbreak of illness, beyond the usual cold and flu season.

While it was strange to see the once-vibrant medina almost entirely stilled, I was aware that there was a lot going on behind the walls of the houses. Artisans and workers who had spent most of their waking lives at their workshops and workplaces suddenly found themselves unable to do anything except wait.

Over the past decade, tourism was steadily increasing, and it had been common to see wide-eyed foreigners seeking their way among the intricate maze of alleys.

I had sometimes cursed the seemingly endless lines of tourists in my narrow local food souk, adding a degree of difficulty to everyday shopping. Now that they were gone, their absence was keenly felt.

It was sad to visit my guesthouse and remember it full of people and life such a short time ago. The need to continue paying bills while my business was shut was a source of stress, but my situation was minor in comparison to what many others in the medina were experiencing.

One of the major groups affected was the craftspeople. Suddenly forced to shut up shop, the artisans now spent their days sipping tea in their studios, playing card games, or talking to their friends.

A decade ago, there were around thirty thousand craftspeople; however, numbers have been declining because of the difficulty of getting apprentices. Most artisans live hand-to-mouth, and the overnight disappearance of their customers was devastating. Even if they wanted to keep producing their crafts, supply lines had dried up.

Closed artisans' shops on the Ta'laa K'bira

"No one can sharpen an awl or a knife," explained my artisan friend Hamza. "You can't buy good-quality leather or brass. The other day, the last man who made leather stamps permanently closed his studio.

"With their studios closed, artisans can't pay their bills. I often pass places with the lights shut off. Banks are offering loans with special deals, but how can they afford to take on loans, when they don't know when this will end?

"At the moment, some craftsmen are making serious decisions to stop crafting. It is a big shock. It is clear that the whole market is fragile. People are looking for other kinds of work."

While the government was giving some emergency support, it was in no way a replacement for the Moroccans and foreigners who had daily trawled the medina in search of handmade treasures.

*   *   *

The state of emergency was due to end on June 10. As the time approached, and along with the prospect of Eid al-Kabir, the most important holiday on the Islamic calendar, a new spirit of hope began to permeate the streets. People appeared and resumed their evening strolls. Cafés and hammams reopened for limited hours, as did some shops.

I was surprised to see artwork appearing on the walls near my house. Near R'cif there was a new mural of King Mohamed VI and emergency service workers on a bright red background. Nearby, a formerly dark, rubbish-strewn tunnel was painted white and adorned with a line of trees.

At the top of the medina, off the Tala'a Sghira, one of the main streets, skilled artists and local teenagers got together to create an open-air gallery that was a celebration of Moroccan culture. Geometric patterns and depictions of traditional Moroccans were the main themes.

"We wanted to give some happiness to the neighborhood, after such a terrible time," said one of the artists.

In the Ziat quarter, a group of teenagers worked for two weeks to beautify their local area. They began by cleaning the streets and re-plastering the battered walls before creating colorful murals.

Local children inspect part of a new mural by Violeta Caldrés

Eighteen-year-old Mohamed said, "Each household gave between fifty and two hundred dirhams for paint and cleaning materials, and everyone supports us."

But not everyone was as supportive. Opinion was divided among the handful of remaining foreign residents and the tourist guides. Some thought it a pity to "deface" the walls of the medina, which had been sand-colored for centuries. Some guides were concerned that tourists would prefer a fifteenth-century-style backdrop for their photos, rather than the new fields of color.

My friend Cathy pointed out that it was likely to be a long time before the tourists returned. "In the meantime, while the residents are suffering through the economic crisis, a little art that occupies people, brings them joy, and opens minds doesn't seem to be a major problem."

I was pleased to see the energy and enthusiasm of the young residents who chose to beautify their city. The Fez medina is a constantly evolving place. Despite its time-travel allure, it is not a museum. It's important to protect history, but a sense of community among the people who live there is the glue that keeps it together.

I hope that sense of community will help overcome the damage an extended lockdown and economic hardship is wreaking on the complex social and cultural ecosystem, developed over more than a millennium.

Fez has weathered many trials over the centuries that were as difficult, if not more so, than the one we are going through now. I love living in a society where warmth, generosity, and tradition are an integral part of everyday life. As we come out from, then go back into, lockdown, I frequently catch glimpses of kindness and humanity in my everyday interactions and know that that spirit endures.

Coming to Grips with Morocco: The Three Stages

by Eirlys Davies

When I first stepped onto Moroccan soil, I had no idea that I would spend many more years in this country than I had spent in my country of birth, England. The journey from being a curious tourist to feeling that I am here for the duration has taken me over forty years, and when I look back on it, I can distinguish three main stages: Revelation, Alienation, and Adaptation.

Stage I: Revelation

I first encountered Morocco on holiday trips. At the time of my first visit, I was living in the north of France, so I left a gloomy, gray town, surrounded by dark slag heaps and all too often wreathed in fog, and took a flight from Paris to Casablanca. Since I arrived after nightfall, it was not until the following morning that I looked out of the window and got my first glimpse of a Moroccan garden. Clementines glowing amidst deep green foliage, rows of canna lilies in scarlet and orange, and a gloriously gaudy hedge loaded with bougainvillea bracts in clashing pink and purple, rust and ruby — the more subtle milky white and faded apricot shades I later grew to love were not in fashion in those days. A symphony of saturated colors, and above them all that luminous, deep blue sky.

As I entered my hosts' large reception room later that morning, the decor seemed to me like a man-made response to that dazzling natural display: a deep red carpet bordered in green, pink and blue brocade upholstery, mustard-colored lacy curtains, gilded wooden tables, and huge sunflower-yellow china vases filled with multicolored plastic flowers. Nature can combine any set of colors; Moroccan interior decorators of the seventies did the same, inventing bling-bling long before the term was even coined.

Morocco was not just a feast for my eyes, but for my other senses too. Everything seemed so extreme. The tea, for someone used to English tea with milk and no sugar, was so cloyingly sweet, so heavily mint-scented. The spice combinations were complex and delicious, but so earthy and pungent that to me they seemed to entirely obscure the taste of the meat they were meant to enhance. On the other hand, the smell from the unrefrigerated product displayed on butchers' stalls was unmistakably, unashamedly meaty.

So much of what I saw seemed larger than life. Up till then, I had known poinsettias as Christmas decorations and rubber trees as spindly indoor potted plants that rarely thrived for more than a few months. I was astonished to find sturdy shrubs covered in those starry crimson bracts, and enormous rubber trees with curious aerial roots that reminded me of elephants' trunks.

Before visiting an outdoor market, I anticipated stalls displaying neat rows of fruit and vegetables; instead, I found whole truckloads of watermelons and oranges simply tipped out onto the ground, in avalanches of green and gold, with shoppers crouched down, scrabbling and prodding in order to choose the best specimens.

Meals I ate in family homes seemed equally off the scale: no individual servings of anything, but vast heaped platters that even twice as many people would not have been able to clear, so that after everyone had eaten their fill, they left the table still heavily laden.

My recollections of the actual events of those seventies holidays are now quite blurred, but my sensory memories are still as vivid as ever. To this day, the combination of blaring car horns, buzzing moped engines, and street vendors' unintelligible shouts transports me without fail to the terrace of a Casablanca apartment where I loved to sit in the sun. One waft of the heady scent of orange blossom, and I am back on a Marrakesh avenue on a sunny spring day. And the chitter-chatter of swallows takes me straight to the gardens of Fez's Palais Jamaï Hotel, where I used to watch them swoop and soar over the swimming pool, skimming the surface with their bellies.

After a few weeks of this colorful, noisy confusion, I would get the same rude awakening each time I landed back in London. Without fail, I would be pulled out of the crowd scurrying through the airport's nothing-to-declare corridor and made to open my suitcase. The customs officer would bend back the covers of a precious book to crack open the spine and check if anything had been secreted there. He would insert a spatula into pots of face cream, unwind the end of my metal toothpaste tube (yes, it was a long time ago), open the lining of my case and search the pockets of all the clothes inside it — although, surprisingly, he never checked the pockets of what I was actually wearing. After enduring this kind of search on several occasions, one day I finally plucked up the courage to ask what he was looking for. He seemed astonished at my naivete. A young female student making repeated solo trips to Morocco? There could be only one explanation for that. I looked at him aghast. My mind was still brimful of memories of rose water, figs, and almond biscuits, and this man thought I had gone there for drugs!

The fact that this idea had never occurred to me before shows how little I really knew of Morocco, even after several holidays there.

My vision of Morocco during this first period was thus one of disjointed sensations, rather than a coherent picture. But when I moved to Morocco to live and work in Fez, in the early eighties, those same sights, sounds, and scents became banal features in the background of my everyday life. In this second phase, the shock was not so much sensory as cultural. Life couldn't continue as a series of fleeting impressions; I had to make sense of it.

And that was far easier said than done.

Stage II: Alienation

The sense of isolation I experienced in 1980s Fez may seem incomprehensible to those who have grown up with Facebook, WhatsApp, and Netflix. Not only was there no Internet, no computer, no video player, but we didn't even have a phone!

I wrote weekly letters to my mother, and if I was very lucky I would get a letter back two weeks later, even though this might well be the reply to a letter I had sent two months earlier.

There was just one Moroccan television channel (but how I envied the residents of Tangier, who with their Eiffel Tower–style rooftop aerials could capture not only Spanish channels but even that of Gibraltar!). The only way I could hear the UK news was via a shortwave radio that, after much coaxing, tapping, and repositioning, would eventually emit the crackly strains of "Lillibullero," the BBC World Service's signature tune. The signal was often so weak I would have to press my ear to the loudspeaker in order to make anything out. But by this means I managed to follow the events of the Falklands War and, later on, the 1991 Gulf War.

When I felt particularly homesick, I would splurge twenty-five dirhams (about two quid) on the *Sunday Times*, which arrived on Fez newsstands on Tuesday or Wednesday, except when the censor had decreed that that week's issue should not be put on sale at all. This purchase seemed to me the height of extravagance, for at the time, Moroccan newspapers cost just one dirham. But reading all the sections from beginning to end, including the advertisements, would soothe my homesickness for several days.

Though I was living in one of Morocco's major cities, I sometimes felt like a castaway on a desert island. When I tried to register to vote in UK elections by completing a form mailed to me by the British consulate, I found it was impossible because I simply did not know a single British citizen in Fez who could provide the required signature confirming my identity!

I had married, and now that I was married to a Moroccan, I needed to infiltrate the mysteries of Fassi society. People were kind and welcoming, but the culture gap was so wide that it was years before I could really decipher their intentions. Visitors to our home would inspect the whole apartment before telling me that my television was too small, my fridge was located on the wrong side of the kitchen, or the curtains I had proudly sewn myself were made of totally inappropriate material. I had never encountered such a conformist society, where norms of behavior and style choices were so firmly endorsed within a particular social group. There was a right way of doing everything, a correct time and place for each event.

At parties, women I barely knew would ask me how old I was and then go on to ask why I was not yet pregnant, sometimes actually caressing my stomach as they spoke. Their intention was to show genuine concern for my well-being, but I found myself wanting to flee the room.

Conflicting politeness systems led to many an embarrassing situation. I had been taught that it was polite, if I was a guest in someone's home, to finish the serving of food set before me. But at Moroccan tea parties, no sooner had I drained my glass of tea and eaten the two or three homemade cakes deposited on my plate than both plate and glass would be refilled. At dinner I would dutifully eat a suitably sized portion of meat, only to find that my kind host then placed a much larger piece before me. There was no choice; I had to go on. Instead of "Would you like a little more?" or even "Help yourself," it was "Eat, eat!"

I was used to the "Don't impose" maxim of Northern European politeness systems, but here the rule was definitely "Don't take no for an answer."

Sometimes I unintentionally triggered this duty of generosity myself. Sitting in someone's formal reception room, I politely (or so I thought) admired an elaborate candle on the coffee table. When I was leaving, my host thrust that same candle into my hands, feeling duty bound to present it to me as a gift, since I had liked it so much. I was mortified!

When our son arrived, I was bombarded with all sorts of well-meaning advice. In the early days I was instructed to swaddle my baby tightly, lest he grow up to have bandy legs. I was told that I should always add sugar to any water I offered him to drink, as otherwise he would find it totally unpalatable. I was advised that I could protect him from choking simply by placing on the top of his head a short length of red wool (obtained from one of those colorful carpets). And when he began to walk and I went to an expensive shoe shop to get his feet measured, so I could buy shoes of the correct width, I was told earnestly by the manager that I should deliberately choose narrow shoes, otherwise his feet would just get wider and wider, and I would have problems finding any shoes to fit him later on!

I slowly learned to hold my tongue and look grateful, and later still I learned to actually feel grateful, even for advice I knew I would never follow, because it was usually offered with care, concern, and a sincere desire to help.

And I also grew more and more conscious of my own frequent misinterpretations. At first, people's behavior sometimes seemed a little scary. The voices of men at café tables were so loud that I often had the impression they were arguing fiercely, when in fact they were merely engaging in amiable chitchat. Unknown women in a crowded street would grasp my arm or tap my shoulder authoritatively, simply because they wanted to get past me. As a relatively untraveled British girl, I found this rather alarming. And it took me a very long time to get used to strangers pressing up against me in queues.

It was so easy to get the wrong end of the stick. For instance, I remember initially being very impressed when I learned that Moroccan women did not take their husbands' surnames on marriage. How liberated, I thought, compared to European women who mostly still stuck to this tradition! However, I was quickly enlightened by one of my students who was soon to be married. A woman preserved her original surname, she explained, not to assert her own independence vis-à-vis her husband, but to show proper respect to the father who had passed this name on to her. The underlying principle was not so different after all — a woman's name must come from a man — but I had been looking at the situation the wrong way round.

Stage III: Adaptation

The years rolled by, and I got along as best I could, but I never quite succeeded in feeling like an honorary Fassia. Even after twelve years living and working in Fez, if I walked down the boulevard alone, young men on mopeds would stop and offer to take me on a tour of the medina. It was not until we moved to Tangier that the third phase of my life in Morocco began. Suddenly I could walk wherever I wanted in the city without attracting the slightest attention from passersby.

Tangier in the nineties was such a cosmopolitan place that its residents were used to rubbing shoulders with all kinds of eccentric and exotic folk and did not appear to judge others by appearances.

In Fez, whenever I had tried to use my still halting colloquial Arabic to a shopkeeper or neighbor, my interlocutors would immediately reply in French. They seemed to find it highly amusing if a foreigner ventured to say a few words in Arabic.

In Tangier, on the contrary, the streets rang with a mixture of Spanish, English, French, and other unidentifiable tongues, and no one seemed to care if you stuck two words in one language beside three in another, as long as the message was conveyed. Even street signs and shop names often featured several languages. Social events were equally varied, ranging from flamenco evenings and book fairs to church fêtes and recitals of Andalusian music, and the curious thing was that you were likely to meet the same people in all these diverse settings.

Tourists visiting Tangier tend to head for the beaches, bazaars, and hotel bars, but the place that soon became my favorite spot for a stroll was the popular flea market of Casa Barata, whose narrow streets were strewn with the castoff possessions of the many nomads who had passed through this once international city, along with goods retrieved from Europe's refuse dumps and transported to Tangier to be sold at a healthy profit. Here you could pick up dusty books in Hebrew or Dutch, solid oak furniture from Belgium, tattered magazines discarded by tourists thirty years ago, German Christmas decorations, and framed black-and-white photos of weddings or first communions celebrated within Tangier's long-established Italian and Spanish communities. The history of the city could be read in this apparently random assembly of objects.

I felt far more at home here than among the flashy beach cafés or city-center shops. For there was a place for everything and everyone in this dilapidated, disorderly yet endlessly fascinating market. Here there was no need to conform, no need to seek to please the majority. I found myself amidst the flotsam and jetsam of so many people whose paths, through a series of chance events, had led them or their possessions to end up just here and nowhere else.

I still wander there and wonder if one day my own unwanted possessions will be on display here. Will anyone buy my books and bric-a-brac? If they do, then maybe I will have added my own little pinch of spice to the melting pot that is Tangier.

Perhaps the moment I really felt I had become part of this chaotic, volatile community came when I caught a taxi to work one morning and spent the journey discussing such topics as the weather, the traffic, the coming summer season, and the recent taxi-drivers' strike — all in colloquial Arabic, with the odd French word if I got stuck. As I paid the driver and got out, he said to me, still in Arabic, "You know what? When I first picked you up, I mistook you for a foreigner!"

I have known a few foreigners who moved to Morocco and underwent something close to a total immersion in Moroccan culture. They changed their way of living, of eating, of dressing, and some even changed their names and gave up on transmitting their native language to their children. Others have remained proud expatriates, enjoying their new surroundings, the climate, the scenery, and leisure opportunities, but remaining very much on the edge of Moroccan society. I do not identify with either of these models. I have just muddled my way through life here, embracing what I could cope with and avoiding what I could not.

While I think I have acclimated to life in Morocco, I can't claim to have really assimilated.

I don't devote any of my time to preparing Moroccan cakes.

I don't look forward eagerly to Eid al-Kabir; to be honest, I don't look forward to it at all!

I don't find myself muttering "insha'Allah" to myself, or fearing that compliments paid to me might make me a victim of the evil eye.

I don't dress in a caftan to attend weddings; indeed, I avoid attending weddings whenever possible, for I have never been able to share the pleasure Moroccans take in spending hours and hours at a party that is too noisy to allow you to chat, too crowded to allow you to circulate, and too drawn-out to allow you to enjoy the banquet, which is not served until three o'clock in the morning.

And yet my everyday life is spent more or less harmoniously among Moroccans. I may not share all their opinions, but at least I understand where they are coming from. I laugh at their jokes, I share their aspirations and frustrations, and I am comfortable in what is, after all, now my normal environment.

When I return to Morocco after a couple of weeks abroad, it takes me a while to stop being irritated by some common behavior patterns: the tendency to drop litter, a very flexible attitude to appointments and deadlines, reckless driving, and a general disregard for rules and regulations. But after such a break, I am also always happy to rediscover Moroccans' delightful willingness to engage with others, their lightness of spirit, and their ability to laugh at almost anything, including themselves.

Morocco has changed almost beyond recognition since I first landed here. Little by little, the world has grown smaller: distances have shrunk, remote corners have grown more accessible, connections are more easily made. Strangers arriving in Morocco today may not feel as mystified as I often did; indeed, they may feel confident that they have got to grips with the place within a few months.

Yet I think that over these forty years, my most important lesson has been that I cannot expect to understand everything. Now I know that I must not look at everything through the lens of my own camera, as that may lead to distorted visions. I no longer expect everything to be in sharp focus, but accept that a blurred impression can sometimes be good enough. Sure, I will never be an expert on Morocco, but I hope I know enough to be able to find my way in this society.

My relationship with Morocco has moved on from the initial encounters, when I was entranced by superficial details, through a long period when I struggled to make sense of a world that often seemed unfathomable, to a point where I have finally worked out a modus operandi I am happy with. Along the way I have experienced many things: exhilaration, desperation, indignation, stagnation. But who knows? Perhaps I would have gone through these same experiences even if I had chosen to make my life in my homeland.

In the end, Morocco is just one corner of the world, not all that different from other corners. Like any other country, it may afford you friends and foes, hopes and heartbreaks, dreams and disappointments. What you ultimately get out of it will probably depend on what you put in. I just hope I have put into Morocco enough to be able to hang on to my friends, my hopes, and my dreams.

Headfirst into the Hammam

by Amanda Mouttaki

The man in the Madrid airport said, "We never saw women when we went out. There were men everywhere but not a woman in sight. Where were they?"

I scratched my head. We were talking about Morocco. He had been there a few times and had noticed the men lining the cafes, out on the street, working in the shops…. But the women? They seemed hidden to him somehow.

It's true there aren't as many women as men on the street, especially in the tourist-heavy medinas of Morocco. They don't take up space in cafes or hawk their wares to passersby. But I also knew exactly where the women of Morocco were. We have spaces — they just often aren't in public view.

Visit any Moroccan home in the middle of the afternoon, and you'll find a group of women chatting over coffee or tea and watching soap operas. Afterward, head to the local hammam, and the sounds of their voices are unmistakable. The neighborhood hammam is an integral part of daily life here, especially for women. This is an entire side of Moroccan life few tourists experience.

Hammams are ubiquitous in Morocco; they are central to old medinas and often built into new developments. On the surface, a hammam is simply a public bath, a place to go and bathe. Even today, with indoor plumbing, many Moroccans still enjoy a weekly trip to the hammam, not for the bath but for the role it plays in society.

My first time in a hammam, I had no idea what I was in for. Had I known what I was in for, my somewhat prudish American self might have said absolutely not. It wasn't until later, when my husband and I moved to Morocco, that I could understand and see the purpose of the hammam in Moroccan life. That first time, though, I didn't know a thing, and the experience will forever be seared in my brain. The only information given was: "You're going for a bath. Bring extra clothes, a towel, and your soap and shampoo."

I was confused, to say the least. Who carries their shampoo around? This was right before my husband and I were married, and the very first time I had met his family in Marrakesh, nearly two decades ago now.

"Come on, yalla, get your things, let's go to the hammam," my soon-to-be sister-in-law chided me.

My other sisters-in-law-to-be pulled their djellabas over their heads and then gathered up buckets and bags and countless other items that somehow were going to translate to this bath.

It didn't take long until we reached an unassuming door with a woman sitting behind a window. It reminded me of how movie tickets used to be sold. I stood there waiting like a lost lamb as my new sisters paid our admission and handed me a glob of some sort of dark, waxy goo wrapped in plastic.

That first visit was akin to having a bucket of cold water thrown on an unsuspecting victim. We beelined for the farthest corner of the changing room, where women were in various states of undress, and I could feel my jaw dropping. The women, who are usually fully covered and quite conservative, had shed all inhibitions when they walked through the door to the hammam. Soon, I too was standing completely in the buff, ready for what awaited me. Every single one of my insecurities was on full display.

There was a cold rush of air as we moved from the changing chamber to the wet rooms. It was only once we stepped inside the wet rooms that I knew I had nothing to worry about.

Women and girls of all ages were sitting in groups, mixed with friends and family. Nobody was sucking in her gut. There was no fear that someone might discover you've got some cellulite on your legs. It didn't even appear to be a thought.

That glob of goo the lady gave me after we paid our admission was black soap. This is a special soap I've come to know well. It's made from olive oil, and you slather it liberally everywhere while you bathe. The heat and the soap loosen up the dead skin. After that, you always remove the loosened, dead skin with a *"kess,"* a glove that feels like tamed sandpaper.

Steam rose from the taps and buckets of hot water sitting on the floor. The scent of olive oil soap and the earthy smell of the ancient walls mingled with the steam, wafting through the chambers. The constant, unbroken chatter was like the comforting babble of a countryside stream, meandering along, following the long curves of life stories and sudden whitewaters of neighborhood gossip. The din was punctured by the odd cry of an angry toddler forced to stop splashing in the water so that their mother might give them a good scrub.

If one of my friends were to be blindfolded and brought into this scene, they might assume they had landed in the midst of some libertine European country. But this was Morocco!

When I had fully lathered, one of my husband's sisters said, "You're ready for the kess," and waved to someone across the room. A woman — who had lived maybe five more decades of life than I — approached me. Aside from a pair of shorts, she was completely naked. We shared no common language at this point, but she pointed at my kess. I nodded. She proceeded to scrub quite literally every inch of my body to the bone, or so it felt. What I thought might be a short, soft scrub was far more intense than I anticipated. She might have been older than me, but there was a rough strength in her that I felt as the kess scratched over my legs and back. She flipped me around like a newborn baby. All I could do was close my eyes and wait for it to be over.

When it was, I was more than ready to call it an afternoon. It had been nearly an hour by then, but I learned I still had to wash my hair and then rinse and then sit and steam longer. I waited for my soon-to-be sisters-in-law to catch up with all their friends — and they had a lot of them!

As I have learned from my years here now in Marrakesh, the hammam is a sacred space. It is where we women come to meet one another, in a male-free zone, to share our stories and our lives. Sometimes mothers are on the lookout for a prospective bride for their sons. Other times, you might find a girl intent on marrying who is seeking information on the brothers of some of the other girls in the neighborhood. This isn't about the physical appearance (though it is a factor) but more about learning who the people are and if they might make a good match. Information passes on the latest happenings in the neighborhood, all while indulging in what is a luxury: uninterrupted time to relax, in the guise of taking a bath. It's true that the importance of hammams as gathering places and matchmaking outposts is starting to fade away, especially in urban areas, where dinner parties or other special events have become more socially acceptable. But wander by any street in any of the old medinas around Morocco, and you're sure to hear the sloshing of water and chatter of women engaged in this time-tested activity.

We had lathered the black soap everywhere. The feeling was slick and rich, and this particular soap had been infused with eucalyptus, adding to the general sense of relaxation and cleanliness. And then we shared these moments together, our lives, our hopes, our dreams, and my future sisters-in-law, well, they caught up with their friends too.

Finally, when it was decided we had had enough of the steam and the conversation, I waddled back to where my clothes were, very happy to be finished. It was a big cultural difference, and I had been thrown in headfirst. Yet nobody else found the hammam awkward, save me. The feeling in the end was one of survival mixed with complete and total relaxation, and the knowledge that I had found a new family. In that one afternoon, I got closer to my future in-laws than in the years I had been with much of my blood family.

In the Madrid airport, I turned back to the man and smiled at the memory of that first hammam. "It's different," I told him. "We women are maybe not where you are expecting us to be, and that's OK. In fact, it's more than OK."

Rootless Plant

by Hazim Azghari

The ultimate goal of farming is not the growing of crops, but the cultivation and perfection of human beings.

—Masanobu Fukuoka

I wish I knew enough Japanese to know exactly how Masanobu Fukuoka worded this. The early people of God said the same thing, or something very similar. Raising crops is not the goal. The goal of farming is something deeper, something rooted within us.

Nature is an aid on the spiritual path. Given enough contemplation, surely the way on this spiritual path can be achieved. The Prophet Muhammed — the last sage, whose favorite color was famously green, a color strongly associated with nature — said, "If the Hour comes and you're planting a seedling, continue to plant it."

*   *   *

Sometimes the feeling of home is not at home, but somewhere maybe not too far from home.

I grew up in an apartment in Morocco's capital city, Rabat, but find myself at home in an eight-hectare farm. It's a long one-hour drive away from the apartment. I say it's a "long" one-hour drive because in this drive, you move from the busy city, with its never-quitting brouhaha, and into the contemplative quiet of the country. In that hour I feel like I've traveled halfway across the world. I feel tired in my bones already. The good sort of tired. The sort of tired you feel after putting in a full day at work and are ready to shuffle off to bed.

"The commute isn't too bad," I am thinking, already planning my move. "I could get home easy. See my parents on the weekend."

I dream about my family moving to the country with me. This way, I might fully sever my ties to the city. "It might happen sometime in the future, insha'Allah," I say to myself, feeling relieved that my attachment is to my kin, not to the house or the city itself.

After that long hour, I get to the farm. It is in the backcountry of Benslimane. People rarely come to Benslimane. The youth usually leave the village to find work in the city. Most of the people who stay here are real salt-of-the-earth types, many of them farmers and farmhands.

Some bits of old-growth forest remain standing, surrounded by the vast stretch of farmland, and not the other way around. "It must have been the other way around before," I think. "This whole world was the other way around before us."

Cork oaks and dwarf palms dominate the forest landscape, interspersed with the occasional sea onion spreads.

A lion was last seen here in the sixties, according to the local newspaper. Did lions live in forests? Did they live here? Perhaps. The images I grew up seeing in documentaries always showed lions in the savannah.

"Maybe this is a savannah," I hazard. "It's not a grassland though."

I gaze across the farmland and the forest, trying to remember. My knowledge of ecosystem classification kicks in. The coexistence of both grasses and trees must make it a savannah. Grasses outcompete tree saplings in a grassland and deprive them of nutrients to grow up, thus dominating the landscape. In forests, trees dominate the canopy and block the sun from reaching the grasses, usually leading to bare ground. The happy medium in between is what has been termed savannah.

Or so we're told.

This might be a classic case of failing to see the forest for the tree, failing to see the wide spectrum of forest diversity for the narrow categories of ecosystems. Or a linguistic cul-de-sac: the word forest traces back to land set aside for hunting. Hunting for wild boars is still practiced around Morocco, but I would not call that hunting per se. Wild boar populations have to be kept in check because otherwise they destroy people's crops, a big problem for unfenced farms. And since there are no more lions to do the job, well, we get guys with guns.

The state issues "hunting" permits for what would be better termed culling, and people happily partake in this necessary cull as if it were a recreational hunt. But it isn't.

People hunt partridges here, too, for food mostly. Ironically, partridges themselves are hard to categorize. Some say they belong to the pheasant family, and some put them under jungle fowl. I digress.

The area of my future home, my farm, is linguistically a forest. Bird taxonomy necessitates an entirely different discussion, and I'm not here to talk about the birds.

What I want to talk to you about is walking between young fruit trees. They don't give much shade, but God provides the rest. Imagination is sparked. How strange is it to walk out to a place where you know you will find the plant, fruit, or vegetable that you need to cook a particular meal?

A farm sometimes feels like an outdoor kitchen to me. It's a strange thought for those of us used to supermarket aisles. I walk between plants, inspecting how everything is changing with the seasons. I almost always find myself picking, chewing, eating. As I walk around the farm, winding up and down the rows, my eyes again glimpse the nearby forest. I try to tell which trees are in season, which fruits are ripe and ready, and then I turn back to the farm and find which vegetables I can pluck from the ground or tear carefully from the vine. Here, I can almost reconstruct a market inventory in my head.

I turn my head to the blue sky. It cuts sharp across the green of the farm and forest. No. This is nothing like a supermarket, but it's where we find a deeper nourishment.

* * *

Years ago I was at a friend's farm outside of Marrakesh. This was one of my first experiences on an organic farm. I remember swimming in the irrigation basin after maghrib prayer as the sun set after a hot day. The breeze whipped around us, cooling us after a long summer day when the sun never ceased to pepper the earth. This breeze and that swim were what made that heat enjoyable, just as, in winter, I later learned the warmth of a djellaba, the traditional Moroccan garb, was what made the cold enjoyable.

I have thoughts as to why I have been so alienated from feeling like a creature — like other creatures of God. Fear, I decide, has a lot to do with it.

I find myself unlearning the art of killing spiders.

I remain calm around dogs.

I am suddenly possessed with the urge to stroke every cat I see.

The heads of cows and horses I still find large, but I no longer think of them as frighteningly gigantic.

This newfound relaxation around these other creatures, God's creatures, has allowed me to discover that fear was keeping me from some admittedly enjoyable acts.

The stroking of a cat I now find verges almost on the spiritual. As spiritual, say, as a warm hug from a beloved friend can be, not to get too New Agey or anything.

The fixation on being sparkling clean, a feeling I usually get when wearing city clothes, is also gone during my time at the farm. These city clothes, or modern clothes if you like, are a rather strange thing for a nature lover to wear. Prone to being stained, needing of ironing once washed, and socially unacceptable in either their stained or wrinkled states. Behind them, an entire steam-engine-powered industry is needed just so they might be donned — though the moment a splash of mud or speck of dirt blemishes their appearance, they must be thrown in the laundry bin.

Rough djellabas and wool kandrissa trousers, on the other hand, are much more low-maintenance. These are meant to have a little mud, a bit of dirt, to be worn many days before chucking them in with the week's wash.

At the farm, I now take water-only showers at night to keep the bed clean and pray sometimes with a bit of mud caked between my toes. This gives me more satisfaction than I can explain here. Gone are the first awkward walks I took there, when I used to worry about staining my shoes, my expensive city shirt, my nice trousers.

Car rides to Rabat felt like an escape into uncharted territory. Sometimes I'd walk in town like a stranger.

"I'm from outside now."

*　　*　　*

My relationship to money has become different.

Coins are no longer counted. God puts a great taste in that snack I bought from the lady in the small shop by the mosque. It's like tasting the worldly reward as a reminder for the otherworldly one to come, insha'Allah.

I also realize that having a conversation with the sellers without buying anything is possible, enjoyable and not something to avoid, as I used to think. The trap is not buying — as critics of capitalism and proponents of #NoBuyDay would make us believe — but failing to connect on a human level, at least while shops and stalls are still manned and not automated yet.

The Shafi'i madhhab, one of the most widespread schools of Muslim jurisprudence, stipulates that a human transaction is necessary for a commercial transaction to be considered valid. One of my teachers repeats this. I think of this as I think of the lady in the small shop. Human transaction.

The car starts to smell nicer as well, as if it were a machine slowly growing roots and degrading the bedrock into soil. It's earthy. The fuss about cleanliness disappears, and the smell of a nicely air-dried pillow is the best to sleep on after having come back to the farm and having enjoyed a light vegetarian tagine like those my grandparents might have had.

Last September, a friend and I organized a retreat on this farm. The experience went reasonably well, if I consider that I met the person who would later introduce me to my lovely wife. There's something deeper here, I think. I first felt it by chance (or by divine plan?). But what is it? What is this feeling I have? This draw toward the green, toward the things buried in the dirt? To the drizzling rain and the blooming flower?

The healing power of nature, some might say. Or maybe the primal connection to working the land, which our ancestors have done for a few thousand years, others might say. I personally think it has something more to do with the need for meaning in one's life.

Some of my generation, millennials, seem to find this feeling by seeking meaning in jobs, which too often takes the shape of impact measurement.

"High-impact startups," I read somewhere.

I am a millennial, but maybe just not this particular kind of millennial.

My search for meaning has made me seek a meaningful process more than measurable impact.

Being on the right path is more satisfying to me than seeing the impact of my work, although it is very important still. It took me a long time to be able to put into words that being on a farm made me feel like I was on the right path. It was very difficult to pin it down, but I could sum it up as those same things Paul Kingsnorth — a "dark" ecologist, for lack of a better way to describe him — considered not to be a waste of his time. After an elaborate critique of classical and postmodern environmentalism, he came to the conclusion that valuing non-human life, getting one's hands dirty, and withdrawing is one path.

The feeling of being on the right path is very tied to the idea of process and not completion.

It is made up of tiny moments, chunks of "right" feelings almost, which come to mind when plowing the soil, digging roots, making compost, but not really when harvesting fruit. It is almost as if the purpose wasn't the fruit, but the benefit one gets from the process of managing nature.

"Managing nature."

An intriguing word combination.

The word management traces back to *ménage*, a household, but nature isn't a household that we are tending to.

"Working with nature" — as is commonly heard in permaculture circles — is not any better, really. Work has a loaded history of bad connotations and in some cases can be the very thing one is withdrawing from when retreating to a farm.

Whatever you call the process — deep ecology, land stewardship or even husbandry — just as long as it does not turn to the other extreme — a cult of productivity — it is this process that refines the soul.

* * *

At last, the hour — not the Hour that the Prophet Muhammed foretold, but the late hour, at which I'm finishing this essay — has come. In a way, I suppose this thing that I'm writing to you is a seed. Its fruit will grow somewhere on, or perhaps within, a rootless plant of flesh and bone to walk the earth and plant seeds of its own. The work itself is the reward.

The Making of a Saint
by Lucas Peters

If you were to travel deep into the heart of the little-visited Souss region of Morocco in the heat of August, you would be privy to a grand spectacle. Nightly chanting by the flickering of fire light, the pious reciting prayers and suras from the *Holy Qu'ran*. Around the campfires, drums beat a steady rhythm, accompanied by the strumming of ouds and watars, and the quick scales of the lghita flute rising above the din, not unlike the slow, swaying rise of a cobra snake, all flickering tongue and piercing eyes. Not far away, goats, cows, sheep, and occasionally a camel are being sacrificed, their meat to be given to the poor. Still others circle a tomb, occasionally kissing it, each praying for a miracle, for salvation, or for good health. They have all gathered here, in Tazeroualte, for the three day pilgrimage to honor Sidi Ahmed ou Moussa, one of the most venerated saints of Morocco.

The history of Moroccan saints is complex. In fact, "saint" is not exactly the correct word, though it is the closest we have in English. There is no "sainthood" in Islam. What is probably most correct is something like "venerated historic religious figure," though it doesn't quite roll off the tongue as easily as "saint."

Sidi Ahmed ou Moussa, is one of the four primary "saints" of Morocco. Every year, tens of thousands of Moroccans make a pilgrimage to his burial site in Tazeroualte. This pilgrimage is dubbed locally as "l'hajj el-meskin," or "the pilgrimage of the poor." For some, the mandatory pilgrimage to distant Mecca is not possible, so this is an acceptable alternative for some. It is a festive, joyous time with many paying their respects and seeking the *baraka*, a sort of holy energy that might ease their lives or the lives of their loved ones. Each person comes seeking this baraka in the hopes that it might prove transformative.

Scant is known about Sidi Ahmed ou Moussa in the English-speaking world. His Wikipedia page is nine sentences long. Even in Morocco, very few know much about the realities of this historic figure. It is known that he was born in 1460 CE and died more than one hundred years later in 1564, in Tazeroualte. In his lifetime, he grew as a powerful leader of his tribe and his spiritual might was feared and respected, even by the sultan of Morocco. What legends and stories we have of him have been passed down through oral stories. Generation after generation of storytellers has taken these stories and most definitely embellished them over the years, adding their own touches and flourishes.

What we know about Sidi Ahmed ou Moussa today is more myth than man. Or perhaps it's more fitting to say that what we know today is that he was a learned man, a powerful man, a spiritual man, and a man who was known, even in his time, to have performed miracles. He made water spring from the desert of Baghdad, wrung a river from the tears of a snake, rode the back of a lion, carried a horse down a mountain cliff, and helped the angels drag the sun across the sky. We also know that he was an acrobat. Historically, acrobatism was a type of entertainment as well as a warrior training for boys.

Above all, perhaps, it is known that he was a kind man. I think there is no story that illustrates this more than the origin story of Sidi Ahmed ou Moussa. What follows is my own translation and interpretation (along with flourishes, embellishments, and the like) of this very story.

The Tale of the Baraka

She hobbled up the hill, aided by a large stick she had found alongside the dusty road. With each step, a sharp pain shot up from her heel, spiking over her calf, wrapping around her thigh until striking directly at the base of her spine. She could see the pain. It was a flash of lightning dashing her vision. Or maybe it wasn't that she could see her pain. It was white and it was blinding. Yes. A blinding pain, she thought. Maybe it would be something she could laugh at later, these momentary pieces of blindness as she scaled the hill. Her heel struck the ground and once again a fresh jolt of pain spiked through her, making her wince, and the whole world flashed white. All thoughts of laughter quickly dissolved. She wanted to stop. Needed to stop. But the figs needed to get to her sister more. She carried the heavy basket of ripe figs atop her head. They pressed down on the crown, compressed her spine, weighing on her aged back.

It had been a tough winter and a tougher spring. After the cold, the big rains had come, washing down the mountains, flooding the valleys and hillsides, rooting out the top soil, destroying much of their crops. If she could just get to the gorge beyond Ilmaten, she knew the family would be okay.

"Please God," she said, taking one more painful step. "Please."

She didn't know what else she might do other than walk and pray. The sun beat down hard, the first real sun of the summer. This was not a winter sun. There was no coldness to it. No. This was the dangerous sun, the one you needed to shield yourself from in the midday or risk falling over, in need of water.

Water, she thought. She would have to stop for water.

Up ahead, a small group of boys walked toward her. They were mere shadows on the horizon, but the old woman could make out the distinct cuts of their costume, the way the shoulders plumed out like two camel humps. They must be coming from the wedding. Her sister had told her that there would be a wedding this week with much celebrating. The groom was a sheep man. The failed crops had not affected him so much. He said it just meant he had to walk farther with his sheep, and he enjoyed walking, so it was not so bad. The bride was from Tindine. It was thought to be a good fit, her sister said. The family in Tindine were known to be honest and hardworking.

As the boys drew nearer, she saw just how young they were. They each carried a small slingshot and small bag of stones. The woman understood. It was dangerous country. There were bandits and thieves. The woman had not thought about that. They were never interested in an old woman. It was the young boys they wanted most. She had heard the stories of boys disappearing. But where would they disappear to? At first, she had thought it might be the work of the jinn. Then she had heard the boys were taken to the North, over the mountains and to Salé, where they were sold and put on ships. Those poor boys, she thought.

There were nine boys in the group. As they came closer, she could make out their colorful costumes in saffrons and ruby reds and from their faces she knew they were from Ilmaten, the village she had just passed through. The gorge was not much further, but with each step, the pain had become almost unbearable, even with the makeshift crutch she clutched with her arthritic fingers. The boys sang as they walked, cheerful and full of smiles. It must have been a good marriage and they must have been paid well, the woman thought. Perhaps they could help me?

As the group of boys came closer, the woman found a piece of shade and put down the basket of figs. She leaned all of her weight on the stick. The pain stopped and she found her voice.

"My refuge and your support, my brothers," she interrupted their song. "Please carry this basket for me just to the gorge ahead."

The boys looked at each other, their slingshots clutched in their hands. Was this some sort of trick? They had heard the stories and their parents had warned them. Boys were being disappeared. It was known. Their eyes scanned back and forth, distrustful. Under the hard sun, there was little else but the quiet. A soft whistle of breeze carried over the dust and rock.

The boys had worked all day and all night. It was hard, physical work, too. They were acrobats. They had formed pyramids and towers with their bodies that reached far into the sky, climbing upon one another, making something incredible from the human form. They banded together in a circle, providing energy and foundation, and they proved their faith through their strength, concentration, discipline and trust in each other, as they climbed on one another, reaching higher and higher until it seemed they could touch the sky. This was part of their training, they understood. They would be warriors and their tribes needed warriors. There was much evil in the world and it was dangerous for boys. They had to stick together. Their unity was their strength.

The old woman with her figs, she would have to find her own way.

The troop of boys shook their heads, one after another. Not a single one of them wanted to even touch her fig basket.

"Please," she begged. The troop of boys began walking on, one boy in the lead picking up where the song had left off.

The woman leaded harder on her crutch beneath the shade, her head bent toward the earth. I can't do this, she said, feeling the truth of it in her bones. I can't do this. She listened as the troop faded into down the hill and into the distance, the melody of their cheerful song fading with them.

"The other boys are scared, auntie," a voice said. "That's all."

The woman looked up, surprised, and saw one of the boys in his bright costume, a slingshot in one hand, a tambourine in the other and a skein of water tied around his waist.

"But you're not scared?" she asked.

"Here I am."

"And so you are." A smile cracked the woman's face.

It had been a hard road for the woman. The boy could see that. He eyed the basket of figs, weighing them in his mind. It would be a heavy load. The figs were ripe, full of their sweet nectary juice, and the road ahead was steep. If they were lucky, they would find some shade to spend the hottest part of the afternoon. If they weren't lucky, well, he didn't want to think about that.

"If you can put your faith in God, auntie, you can put your hope there, too," the boy said.

"And so you can," the woman responded.

The boy untied the skein from his waist and gave it to her. She thanked him and took a long gulp. The water was cool and fresh and sweet. He encouraged her to drink some more and then took back the skein and tied it back to his waist. He handed the old woman his tambourine and slingshot, wrapped a turban over his head and lifted the basket of figs, resting them delicately atop the turban. They were not so unlike Hamid, his friend, how the weight of them rested easily, naturally settling and finding their way around the shape of his skull. Hamid had stood upon his shoulders, his weight resting just as easily as the basket of figs. He walked across square with Hamid balancing on his shoulders to the bride and groom. He stopped not two lengths from the happily married couple, the bride and groom glittered with sequins and silver, golds and silks. All eyes of the festival were on them as Hamid bent at the knees. He felt Hamid shifting his weight, pressing deep into his shoulders before Hamid leapt into the air. He twirled and spun through the air, deftly landing cat-like on his bare feet without a sound. The boy had watched Hamid do this a hundred times but every time he was amazed. Hamid was gifted. He took pleasure in the deep gasp of the audience as Hamid launched into the air, the quick quiet that followed, and then how a sudden thunderstorm of laughter and applause broke that quiet.

As they walked on, the sun beat done, growing hotter by the minute. There was no shade but the gorge was not so far, he thought. Maybe they wouldn't have to rest. The woman walked alongside him, whispering prayers, clutching his slingshot and tambourine in one hand and the knobby olive branch she used as a crutch in the other. The figs began to sweat, their secret, cloudy liquid gathering around their skins, slowly seeping to the bottom of the basket, over the boy's turban and down his face. Rivulets of fig juice mixed with beads of sweat on his cinnamon skin. He looked back at the woman.

"Auntie," he said, "will you be okay?" The question forced out between deep breaths.

The woman did not stop and she did not respond. She continued walking, all the while whispering her prayers.

"Auntie?" he repeated. She continued on, seemingly unaware of him or even the rocky path beneath her feet and the heat of the sun that squeezed down on them. Her breathing was not heavy and she had barely broken a sweat, but her eyes — the boy could see the pain there. With every step, it gathered in the corners. He could see it drain from the corner of her eyes, to the back of her jaw before she clenched her teeth and swallowed it, taking another step.

"My brother," the old woman said. "It's not so bad. Don't you worry about me. You're doing me and my family a great favor." She came closer as she said this.

"But auntie," the boy pleaded. "You need rest."

"What I need is to get this basket to my sister. And then I can rest."

"Are you sure, auntie?"

"This pain is nothing. I have lived through much worse than this."

The woman pressed on in front of him, her uneven steps and makeshift crutch scraping on the dirt and stone, continuing her prayers muttered beneath her shallow breath. The boy followed her up into the hill and to the summit of the gorge and then down into the gorge and to her sister's house. The boy darted his eyes up to the sky. There was still just enough light for him to make it back home, though on the return journey he would be on the road all alone. He would not have Hamid or any of his other friends or even the old woman to keep him company. He was scared, but he did not want to tell the woman this.

He sat the basket of figs down in front of the sister's door and unwrapped his turban. He used the turban to wipe the sweat and fig juice from his brow. When he was done, he rewrapped the turban on his head. The woman handed the tambourine and slingshot back to him. He took them, nodding his head in thanks.

"My son," the old woman said, "oh my son… all along this road I have said these prayers for you. Your good fortune is guaranteed."

The boy looked back up to the sky. Now that the hottest part of the day had passed, he could feel a slight coolness on the breeze. But there was something else, something close to him now that wasn't there before, some shift of nature or maybe something more powerful and he knew the woman's words to be true.

He wished the woman and her family well. As he left, he heard the woman rap her knuckles on the door and the door open. There was a happy greeting full of heartfelt thanks. It was old woman's sister at the door. A guest of wind blew her soft voice across the gorge. "Who is the boy?" she asked.

He walked back up to the summit of the gorge, their eyes hot on his back. He could only make out the one word: baraka.

The boy wanted to turn around then, but he didn't. Something held him back, kept him on the road, forcing him to put one foot in front of the other, his eyes ahead of him as he mounted the steep incline to the summit of the gorge. The road was dangerous and it would be dark soon. His father and mother would be worried.

There was much evil in the world, he knew, but there was good too. He knew this just as he knew the weight of the old woman's basket on his shoulders and the feeling of fig juice as it dripped down his brow, mingling with his sweat. He could hear the sound of his father's voice now. "Ahmed! Why are you so late? We've been worried." And he would tell his father and his mother the story of the lady he helped home with her figs and how he got his baraka.

*　　*　　*

I wanted to share this story of Sidi Ahmed ou Moussa with you. As it turns out, his family, many generations after his passing, has become my family. It was only a couple of years ago I found this little nugget of family history out. I had known that two of my wife's uncles were acrobats in circuses around the world, and that her great grandfather had performed in the very first Ringling Brothers circuses in the United States. However, it wasn't until a chance phone call while I was in the Souss on a travel junket that Amina had told me her connection with this Moroccan saint.

"I can't believe you never told me this!" I said. The connection was bad. I was driving through the Anti-Atlas Mountains toward Tazeroualte. Her voice cracked in and out. Though not perfect, this connection was a comfort as I drove the twisting roads I had never before explored.

"Right?" she said. "I can't believe it either."

"So our son? This means he's some sort of… what exactly?"

"Who knows?" she said. "Maybe this means he'll join the circus, too."

Our son was nearly two years old and had already mastered the somersault. As the car climbed the mountain pass, I pictured him at the mausoleum in Tazeroualte, his chubby arms and legs flailing through the air, channeling the history that flowed within him, learning his place on the human pyramid.

"I hope so," I said. "The world needs more acrobats."

The phone cut out. Our time was up.

A *Memoir* of Home
by Zakariaa Aitouraies

There is this joke they say about Moroccan students like me who study English. It goes: "No matter how hard you try; you cannot convince Moroccan English students that they're actually Moroccans."

I have been thinking about this and have come to the realization that, to some extent, it's true. As far as I can remember, I have always been interested in what's going on outside of my country and my culture. I do not watch Moroccan movies and I hardly ever listen to Moroccan music. And, it pains me to admit, all the books I have read, except for the Qu'ran, are books in English. I feel that I can say the same about most of my former classmates.

Some of them not only did not feel like they were Moroccans, but truly wished they were not.

One of our professors, during our last year, had noticed this and put us to the test.

"I want you to write an essay about what makes you Moroccan," Professor Z said. "It's due next week."

It's my habit to think as deeply as I can about things. I wanted to think about this prompt and look at it in a way that my fellow students would not.

I thought about it for the entire week but I failed. I could not write a single word about what made me Moroccan. I could not come up with an answer. I could not conjure a single word. I have thought about this failure ever since.

You should probably know that, as a matter of fact, the dissertation for my Bachelor's degree concerned the subject of Identity. I suffered just trying to fathom my own, a young man from two worlds, two languages, and I at the intersection. Wordless. Speechless. The irony was not lost on me.

It has been a few years. I'd like to try to go back to Professor Z and answer that question now.

What makes me Moroccan?

Is it the mere fact that I was born and raised here in Morocco? Is it the property of my ID card or my mailing address? Is it the fact that sometimes I get goosebumps when I hear the national anthem (though less as time goes by)? Is it the fact that I think Fridays are not really Fridays without couscous? Is it the dream that I share with all Moroccans of seeing our national team win the World Cup? Is it my language? It can't be. I speak English just as much as I speak Darija. I even reached the point where most of my thoughts are in English. I can express myself and my thoughts in English better than I can in Darija.

Or is it something else? Is it perhaps the sum of all those elements?

At this point, I've realized, as you probably have as well, that I am no longer asking myself the question of "what makes me Moroccan?" but more, "Who am I exactly?"

Months have passed. I graduated, published my first book; a collection of short stories and poems, and started teaching English. It was around this time when an answer came to me. It was not my language, how I felt, or my culture that gave me the satisfaction to finally call myself Moroccan, although they made up a great part of who I am. It was actually a decision I had made a few years ago: to go backpacking in some isolated parts of North Morocco. I left everything behind and took only my phone, which, for most of the time, was dead. I went with a friend of mine and we spent the first six nights in a mountain near Chefchaouen. We met a young man there who came all the way from Marrakesh. He told us that he goes backpacking in the North almost every year. I admired that about him. We let him lead the rest of our trip. This pleased him rather well, so, he decided to take us to a village that neither of us had seen before. The village was called *El Qalaa*, which means *The Castle*. We hiked for about five hours to reach one of the simplest, yet most beautiful, places I had ever seen. The village was utterly surrounded by mighty green mountains and stretched wide. The moment we arrived, we were met with welcoming eyes. Our new friend was immediately recognized.

"Hey! You're that guy from Marrakesh," a stranger said to our new friend. "Thank you for visiting us again. It's lovely to have you here with us. If you and your friends need anything, let us know."

Thank you for visiting. It's lovely to have you.

I repeated these words in my mind. The stranger spoke those words with such sincerity that not only did we feel welcomed, but at home. We built our tents in one of the residents' land, which had been recently harvested. I deliberately walked on the dead straw. Feeling it crack under my shoes filled was a great pleasure. It was evening by then, and once settled, I sat down by my tent and watched the sun sink slowly behind one of the mountains. When night fell, the star-studded sky seemed so close it felt as though one could touch it if only they stretched their arm out enough. The emotions swirling inside me in that moment were indescribably surreal. I was certain that had I been anywhere else, even if the place were infinitely more beautiful than this one, I would not have felt the same. This is what it feels like to belong to a place, to a country, a people. It felt like home.

I wrote a short story, "The Castle," about that small village. There is one cafe, one mosque, and two or three shops that sell almost all necessities. The story is less about The Castle than about the people who welcomed us and gave us bread and olive oil almost every day we spent there. It's a story about that feeling of finally reaching deep into your roots and connecting with who you are and where you belong.

We spent four days in The Castle, the evenings of which were spent mostly in the cafe. Uncle Abdeslam, the owner, served the sweetest coffee and tea you could ever taste. The drinks were mostly sugar. When you finished them, your lips would become sticky. There was an old pool table, morbidly unbalanced, but we still had some fun with it. Every now and then, a young man would approach us and ask if we needed some hashish. Our new friend from Marrakesh would buy some every evening. When he did not have the money, he was given some for free, or he would trade it for something he no longer wanted.

A friend of mine told me once that it's wonderful how we can find some pieces of us in the kindness of others. I've finally come to know what that means now. To truly know oneself, one ought to know and connect with his fellow man.

I remember feeling almost the same way about my hometown a couple of years ago. I was born and raised in a small town eighty kilometers east of Casablanca. It's about an hour drive but the cultural difference is rather distinguishable. Ben Ahmed is mostly a rural place. Its inhabitants mainly come from the villages around it. There are no malls or movie theaters, and for the entire time I had lived there, we didn't even have a supermarket. We had only two schools. I do love that wretched place where I grew up. I even loved its rough people who frowned at almost anything modern that threatened them with change. The walls of almost every street had seen me run through them. My parents still live there; I do my best to visit them at least once a month.

One day I was waiting for the bus that would take me back to Mohammedia, a city just north of Casablanca, where I now live. The bus station was more or less just a large street where busses stopped and took off. A few vendor carts scattered around selling mint leaves, orange juice, popcorn, sweets, and more. Each cart owner shouted, inviting people to buy his product. Ticket sellers howled names of cities too, trying to lure any potential passenger to buy tickets from them.

"Casa! Casa!" One shrieked.

"Berrechid! Berrechid! Who's going to Berrechid?" Shouted another.

There were beggars stretching their hands to people passing by.

I basked in the middle of all the bustle until, in my mind's eye, everything slowed down, coming nearly to a standstill. I could see everything: a boy trying to escape from his mother's hand to buy popcorn; a stray dog resting in the shade of a pickup truck; a woman checking her purse inside the taxi as it drove by; I saw how everyone was just busy, busy doing their best to get to where they were going, whether they knew that place or not. Everyone toiling away, stoically. Busy, busy, busy; moving incessantly, not daring to halt for perhaps, if they had, they might have noticed how miserable life is. Misery, to them, only existed when they paid attention to it. That was the reason why I fell in love with my hometown all over again. That was the reason I felt I belonged there. Most of the people there, no matter how harshly life had treated them, were still moving along with it. It abated some of their pain, I believe. Perhaps it even made them forget it.

We are strangers most to ourselves. We are foreigners in our own lands. Who among us can say, with the utmost confidence, that they know who they are? It's not quite clear to me how we can make such an effort to know others, and so very little to know ourselves. It's not quite clear to me why, as time passes by, and opposite to what one might think, we become strangers in our own homes. It's tragic. We spend years not knowing who we are and living in places without actually being anywhere. I'm doing my best these days to know who I am better, to fall in love with everything that makes me myself, and to fall in love again with the place I belong. In all honesty, I am not there yet, but I can't wait to say to myself the same words the stranger in the village had said to us when we arrived: "Thank you for visiting. It's lovely to have you."

Nothing Is Certain
by Richard Hamilton

There's a saying in Morocco: "Nothing is certain, but everything is possible." The way things have unfolded for me seems to bear that out.

I had not intended to go to Morocco at all. I work as a radio journalist for the BBC World Service, and in 2006 they were advertising two correspondents' positions in Africa: in Uganda and Morocco. I actually wanted to go to Uganda. But my boss said I spoke better French than the other successful candidate, so she went to Kampala, and I found myself in Rabat.

When I arrived, things were quite difficult. I hardly knew anyone in the city, and since it was Ramadan the streets were very quiet during the day. I was renting a particularly soulless apartment. There was no Internet — just a television with endless satellite channels in Arabic, interspersed with the odd French chat show and Italian porn. The apartment also had very small windows, one of which looked out onto the wall of another building about two meters away. It felt like a prison. It was a comfortable enough prison, of course, with one of those soft red Moroccan divans that lined the walls, forming a U-shape. It would have seated about twenty people, but for one person it seemed a sort of social snub of the cruelest kind, an ironic reminder of my solitary life and friends I did not have.

I sent a desperate email to a previous BBC correspondent asking for her advice. She told me that the great advantage of Ramadan was that you ate lots of delicious harira. Although she was undoubtedly right, this was slim comfort. She also mentioned a veteran Reuters correspondent, who she said had been the social hub for Moroccans and expatriates living in Rabat.

"The only problem," she added, "is that he's dead."

So armed only with the prospect of soup and the ghost of a Reuters reporter, my life in Rabat began.

The year 2006 was not long after the invasion of Iraq. George W. Bush's catchy-but-dumb "War on Terror" was still in full flow. In early 2007 another BBC reporter was kidnapped in Gaza, and starting out as a Western journalist in an Arab country filled me with anxiety.

One day after Ramadan I decided to go for a walk in the medina. I was taking photos of the fruit sellers in the market when a man grabbed a large gray gas canister and pretended to fire it at me as if it were a machine gun or an improvised explosive device. It gave me a fright, and I scuttled back home to my empty divan and small windows. There was not much news to report and not much happened in those early weeks.

One thing that did happen was that my credit card got blocked. I rang my bank. They informed me that they would send a new one to London. I kept explaining that this would not help me much, as I was living in Morocco. I grew so angry with the woman in the call center that she became rattled, and at one point, instead of addressing me as "Mr. Hamilton," she called me "Mr. Morocco." Now I quite like that name and think it would look good on my passport.

Some days later I was invited to a drinks party in Rabat by one of the few people I knew. I remember sitting in a taxi as it swerved through the traffic alongside the medieval ramparts of the city, which were lit up in the evening, and I thought what a beautiful place it was. The Islamic architecture, the dark velvet sky, and the lonely crescent moon were breathtakingly beautiful. At that party I talked to a Spanish web designer who told me he was recording stories from the storytellers in Marrakesh, and the videos would be embedded in a website for UNESCO. This gave me an idea for a BBC report, and I set off for Marrakesh.

I took a train from Rabat that seemed to travel no faster than a sluggish camel. I listened to Crosby, Stills, Nash, and Young's "Marrakesh Express" and sat there watching the landscape through the window change from green to yellow, as it became hotter, more arid and mountainous. I was slowly falling in love with this country.

* * *

When I arrived in Marrakesh I met my wife, who had flown in from London, and we looked around for our hotel in the medina. It was as if we had been transported two thousand years back in time. It felt as if nothing had changed. There were donkeys, vegetable sellers, hole-in-the-wall kiosks lit by oil lamps, the smell of spices and the sound of the muezzins echoing from the mosques. It was a complete sensory overload, and I will remember it for the rest of my life.

The next day I interviewed a storyteller. He was an old man called Moulay Mohamed el Jabri. I sat down with him and a translator, Ahmed, in the main square, the Jemaa el-Fnaa, in front of one of the city's oldest colonial establishments, the Café de France. From here I could see the pink walls of the city, the Koutoubia Mosque, and the square's panoply of entertainers, fortune-tellers, acrobats, fire-eaters, and musicians. I remember thinking there was nowhere else in the world I would rather be.

Moulay Mohamed started telling me a folk tale about a poor man who owned a red lantern. I was too impatient to listen to the whole story and pressed on with the interview. But to cut a long story short, some time after I did my radio report, Ahmed turned to me and suggested I write a book about the stories of Marrakesh. So even after my BBC posting was finished, I flew back to Marrakesh many times to finish collecting stories. But at no point could I find Moulay Mohamed. Ahmed did introduce me to other storytellers, who are a dying breed. Then on my last trip Ahmed said, "I've got someone you should meet." It was Moulay Mohamed, and he finished telling me the tale of the red lantern. This is now the opening story in my book *The Last Storytellers: Tales from the Heart of Morocco*. I recorded dozens of tales from four other storytellers that fill out this collection of translated Moroccan oral stories.

One of these storytellers was Abderrahim el Makkouri. We spent many pleasant hours inside the Café de France recording his stories. Abderrahim was hoping his teenage son Zoheir might become a storyteller too. A German filmmaker produced a documentary about them, which was shown at the Marrakesh International Film Festival. But Zoheir could not cope with his sudden exposure to fame and began to experience panic attacks. His mother and father would be woken by his screams in the night. They had to take him out of school and struggled to pay for his medication.

I had an idea. If Zoheir recovered, maybe he could tell stories in the square, I suggested one day, as we sat on the veranda of the Café de France.

"Look," said Abderrahim, "can't you see? There's no space for storytellers anymore," pointing at the crowded stalls of merchants selling everything from mystical aphrodisiacs to false teeth. "And anyway, it's too noisy."

When I returned home I wrote a letter to the royal palace, more in hope than expectation, explaining to the King's advisers that Abderrahim was in dire straits and needed somewhere to tell stories, to save this ancient oral tradition from oblivion.

I went back to Marrakesh later and found out that a new venue called Café Clock had opened. Here the art of storytelling is being revived, with young Moroccans learning ancient tales from the older generation. I arranged to meet Abderrahim again in the café to tell him the good news.

"I have some good news too," he said. "The King got your letter and has bought me a house!"

I was amazed, but then that Moroccan saying came into my head: "Nothing is certain, but everything is possible." Marrakesh is the strangest place I know. Truth here is stranger than fiction. Where else can you buy aphrodisiacs and false teeth? Where else can you hear stories that are older than the pink walls of this medieval city? And where else does the king end up buying a storyteller a house?

* * *

A few years later I decided to write a second book, about one of Morocco's other great cities: Tangier. I knew several famous writers had lived here in the 1950s, but I had no idea until I started researching the book that a whole array of other fascinating characters and oddballs also ended up in this seedy seaport by the Straits. The great diarist of the Fire of London, Samuel Pepys, lived in a house here in 1684 after the British King, Charles II inherited Tangier as party of his dowry from Catherine of Braganza.

I spent four years making annual trips to Tangier, walking the streets in search of its literary, artistic, and musical ghosts. It was a fascinating, if sometimes frustrating, time trying to unlock its deepest, darkest secrets.

After a few ill-fated attempts, I succeeded in entering Pepys' house in the Kasbah. In the courtyard, there is a fig tree that is more than three hundred years old, under which he wrote some of his later notes and diaries.

Some of the other famous Tangerines include Ibn Battuta, who travelled three times further than Marco Polo; Walter Harris, who wrote for *The Times* newspaper, (recording the era before French colonial rule); and Henri Matisse, who painted breathtakingly beautiful canvases inspired by the colors and the light that bounces off two great bodies of water: the Mediterranean and the Atlantic. There was also a wave of American writers, such as Paul Bowles and William Burroughs — who each wrote one of the greatest novels of the twentieth century while living in Tangier, *The Sheltering Sky* and *Naked Lunch, respectively*. Jack Kerouac, Truman Capote, and Tennessee Williams all came here in the 1950s because it was a unique place at a unique time when the city was part of an international zone. It was a sunny place for shady people. But it was also a remarkable experiment in people living together that has rarely been replicated since.

The last chapter of my book is about the founder of the Rolling Stones, Brian Jones, who stayed in Tangier and incorporated ancient Moroccan music into his mixes. He was ahead of his time, before "World Music" was coined by the likes of Peter

Gabriel and Youssou N'Dour. Because my book charts the history of the city from its early times, I've called it *Tangier: From the Romans to the Rolling Stones*. Like Marrakesh, there are no obvious outstanding monuments in Tangier, but its walls reek of history.

The last pages are set in Tangier's Café Hafa, from where you can gaze down on the Mediterranean, across the Straits of Gibraltar, and towards the opaque outline of the Spanish coast. Here you can sip sweet mint tea in one of the most beautiful places on Earth. If Marrakesh is a city of red and pink walls, Tangier is a city of white buildings set against a blue sky and sea. You can imagine why so many artists, writers, and musicians gravitated here.

When I sit in the Café de France in Marrakesh or the Café Hafa in Tangier, contemplating the beauty of this wonderful country, I am glad that uncertain things happened to me, and that I did not go to Uganda.

My Country(wo)men & Artisans

text and photos by Amina Lahbabi

We Moroccans often dislike having our pictures taken by strangers — unless a little banter, a conversation, or a true interest in our culture and who we are precede the act. Even with this all this said, a police request if often required. With the rise of visual media, some still remain skeptical about the use of their image and the description 'exotic'. For someone like me who likes to capture unique emotions and stories through candid street photography, this can be a bit challenging. It wasn't always this way; but as Morocco has welcomed more and more travelers over the decades with their cameras, many of them unfortunately quite aggressive, this constant picture-taking has probably taken a toll on the average Moroccan who just wants to go about their life without having some stranger clicking away in front of their face. Even for a Moroccan, taking pictures around Morocco can be difficult, particularly taking photos of women.

Morocco is truly unique. What makes it most unique are the people you meet along the way, the people that welcome you into their homes, the people that you share a mint tea and a laugh with, the people whose memories live on through their stories wafting up the sky along with the sweet scent of orange blossoms.

The people who make up Morocco are living stories of the cultural crossroads we are born into. We are defined by our relaxed Mediterranean lifestyle, our strong Amazigh character, our gleeful desert attitude, our African sense of togetherness and whatever else that the Arabs, Jews, Europeans, Romans, Phoenicians and many others sprinkled on this beautiful land.

We are all of that and more. The people of Morocco will often share stories of their lives with you at the first encounter just like different cultures before shared their stories with the original inhabitants of this land.

Through photography, I keep trying to capture these stories, these encounters with my fellow country-people.

What follows is a selection of a few of these moments, stolen, volitional, otherwise volatile…

Hamza is a devout Muslim, a loving father of three, and a man who truly believes in the equality of women and men. "Every Friday, I come here for the noon prayer. This is my favorite spot to find solace when I need it. The world is too crazy and sometimes we lose sight of what really matters, like good relationships and love."

Madrasa Bouanania, Fez

Haj Ahmed's cataracts are taking over his vision but he won't give up learning and writing. "For forty years, I have been coming to the same mosque, warming up my bones in the sun at the same doorstep to write down verses of my poems. The rhythm keeps me on my toes, and the rhyme sways me like a gentle breeze."

Meknes

Aisha (or *Mmi* - mama - Aisha as everyone calls her) is a true matriarch. She runs her household like a true logistics manager, cooks for the whole family and helps her husband farm their little patch of land. "I like to come out here to this rocky patch for a breather, because my grandchildren find it too difficult to follow me *laughs*... I wish I had gone to school, but I do know how to make silk buttons. With every thread I write my story."

Imouzzer

Tata comes from the beautiful Ziz Valley oasis where date palms and a panoply of fruit trees droop for whoever walks by to delight in. Tata epitomizes the generosity of the simple and expansive landscape surrounding him. He enjoys inviting people over for a meal in the valley and for tea in the desert. "I am a man of the desert. The vastness and the quiet of the sand dunes are the best music."

Merzouga

Moulay Cherif has been selling nougat for over thirty years. His craft is a lifetime of memories making treats with his father, experimenting with different flavors, and sharing pieces of these with passersby. He takes pride in the longtime tradition. "This is not just a craft but a window into the world. I have met so many people and have learnt so much about places near and far without even leaving my small shop."

Fez

Yto loves the Saturday market in town. Going there means you can find all sorts of things handmade, and Made in China or Turkey, as well as other sorts of produce that her family doesn't grow. "It's a long trek, but well worth it. My favorite is camel milk that the merchants bring from the South."
Tighassaline, Middle Atlas

Said has two camels: Jimi Hendrix and Bob Marley. Said is the eternally happy sort of personality. He loves his camels and says they need to *always* be treated with respect. "They have different personalities, you know. Jimi is very outgoing. But Bob is too shy to be in the photos, so I don't put pressure on him to join in."

Tinghir

Sidi Hafid was one of two last two craftsmen in Fez making traditional wooden buckets once used in hammams. The burgeoning restoration of riads for tourists helped to keep his craft alive. Like many senior artisans in Morocco, he was passionate about his work. "These buckets are way better than plastic ones. I worry, though, that after I'm gone, this craft will go with me. Young people today do not care about continuing the tradition because the modern consumerist world is too alluring."

Sidi Hafid passed away in 2017. R.I.P

Fez

Abdelwahed has a true love story. One he shares with the world without even using words. Abdelwahed has spent his life with Andalusian music. If you walk past the club, you can hear the beautiful strumming of Oud, the steady beats of darbouka, the metallic rattling of a tambourine, and the mellow tunes of violin.

"My fellow musicians and I come to play at the club every day, except on Sundays. Our passion for Arab-Andalusian music is boundless. Nothing and no one can take it away from us."

The Sons of the Strait for Arabo-Andalusian Music Club, Tangier

Him I do not know. I had never seen him before but I knew he had been in that square for a very long time. I never talked to him but I knew he was not in it just for the money. I sat there one evening and watched him play his guembri, transported away from the cacophony and the bustle of Jemaa el-Fnaa… mesmerized by the monotonous melody reminiscing about our African descent.
Marrakesh

Gratitude from the Windy City of Essaouira

by Lynn Houmdi

I arrived in Morocco for what turned out to be a twenty-seven month stay at the start of September 2012, just as the unrest of the so-called Arab Spring was dissipating (or being quashed) throughout North Africa. For the previous year and a bit, I had been traveling between my hometown of Edinburgh, Scotland, and Essaouira, Morocco, every two to three months. These frequent trips were to meet someone I had met during the 2011 Gnaoua World Music Festival, for which Essaouira is known. Our relationship had become much more than a holiday romance. Now I was taking the plunge and moving to Africa!

An opportunity had arisen to request a voluntary redundancy package from my career in the UK civil service. I had been hoping and waiting for three years to qualify. It hadn't looked likely I would, and I spent my lunch breaks dreaming up escape routes and business start-up plans. Then, in the absurd way that government works, on the cusp of a referendum on Scottish independence, my position as Head of UK Relations was merged with another role. With my job being struck off an ever-tighter departmental budget, and having a convincing story about being perpetually separated from my partner in Morocco, suddenly I was considered eligible for the payoff, and you couldn't see me for all the dust in the Sahara.

However, I couldn't leave immediately. So during my final six months as a UK government official, I developed a plan to change my life completely. My plan, at its base, was very simple:

(1) Take the first flight to Morocco.

(2) Live with my love.

(3) Start a small bed-and-breakfast.

I had cash. I had enthusiasm. And I was determined to acquire the skills.

Also, I certainly wasn't going to say no to three hundred–plus days of sunshine a year!

So it was, on an otherwise unremarkable weekday in September 2012, while my former colleagues continued to unpick disputes between the UK and Scottish governments, that I jetted off from the Edinburgh airport for a new life in Morocco.

I landed in Marrakesh to a text message from my partner to say he was on his way. I was about to learn my first Moroccan lesson: patience.

While I waited for him, I engaged in the national occupation of people watching while sitting outside the airport. Taxis and tour buses sped through the arrivals and departure. I looked at each one in anticipation, anxious to begin anew.

As I was to learn, not much happens very quickly in Morocco. Coming from the UK, where every minute of every day was accounted for, I had to adjust to waiting like this.

About an hour and a half later, over dinner, I found out the reason for the delay.

My partner had travelled up to Marrakesh on the 6 a.m. bus from Essaouira with a friend who has a vehicle rental agency. The friend had a new car to collect in Marrakesh, and the plan was that they would be finished in time to collect me in the late afternoon at the airport, in the new car.

It seemed a good plan. I knew Moroccans drive a hard bargain, but surely it didn't take a whole day of haggling to agree on the price of a car? I had forgotten that other national occupation in Francophone Africa: bureaucracy.

The purchase of the car was apparently relatively simple. The time-consuming part had been getting the requisite papers to register, insure, and actually own the car. This involved traveling across Marrakesh, papers in hand, to queue and collect *cachets* (rubber stamps) and scribbled signatures. In over-40°C (100°F) heat.

A third national occupation in Morocco is hospitality. Often, someone you may have met only once would be happy to welcome you into their home and offer you what they have, no matter how little. Luckily for the guys, our car-purchasing friend had a contact in Marrakesh who was able to offer them lunch, a cold shower, and space for a siesta while they waited for the city bureaucrats to do their thing.

So it was that by the time I arrived in Essaouira, tired but happy to be there, our day had already offered a snapshot of what I came to know intimately during my life in Morocco: interminable bureaucracy and lots of waiting, both made all the more palatable by the helping hands and hospitality of friends. On that day, my partner and his friend introduced me to a proverb I have heard many times since in Morocco:

"Europeans have watches, but Africans have time."

My New Home and Family

The history and the destiny of Essaouira, formerly known as Mogador, lie in its location on the Atlantic Ocean. It has, however, more recently achieved fame as one of the locations for the TV series *Game of Thrones*, which transformed the town into a film set while I was living there.

Nestled in a bay protected by an archipelago of uninhabited islands, Essaouira is sheltered from the trade winds that have brought visitors, goods, and traditions from across the world — and likewise transported them onwards. It doesn't feel very sheltered when attempting a beach walk while the wind blows sand horizontally into the face. In summer, however, compared to the sweltering heat inland, the breeze is a blessing. Elhamdulillah.

Arabic is replete with "Allah phrases," as I call them, and they are key in an Islamic society like Morocco.

Elhamdulillah literally means "thanks be to God," or a more secular expression might be "thank goodness," and it peppers every conversation between Moroccans.

The automatic way in which Moroccans use this phrase, I believe, demonstrates their innate gratitude. They don't just use it to be grateful for their own good fortune; it is used as a reminder of those less fortunate than themselves. In many instances, a better translation would be "I am grateful; it could be worse." So when enquiring after someone's health, they will always reply, "Elhamdulillah," no matter how they are feeling. Even when catastrophe strikes, a Moroccan expresses gratitude that the situation isn't even more disastrous.

Life in Essaouira was seldom disastrous but nonetheless not always easy. But I had plenty to be grateful for, not least the welcome I received from my partner's family and friends. I was always included in festivities, such as Eid al-Adha (the festival of sacrifice) and ftour (the meal to break the fast during Ramadan) and was usually fed to the point that they would leave me in the guest salon with a blanket and some cushions to have a little nap.

Learning About the Past

I can also say elhamdulillah for all the friends and connections I made in Essaouira and the insight they gave me into the history, culture, and lifestyle of local people.

While working with the High Atlas Foundation in Essaouira, I was responsible for managing this US-Moroccan nonprofit's first intercultural heritage project. The aim of the project was to use the multicultural and multi-faith (Christian, Jewish, and Muslim) history of Essaouira to educate the younger generation of Moroccans in the lessons of peaceful cohabitation in the past. Many people are still surprised to learn of Morocco's significant Jewish history, in which Mogador, as it was known, played a prominent part.

Through this work, I met Asher Knafo, author, educator, and son of Mogador, who had left with his family in 1951. I accompanied him as he transcribed the rich data of the tombs in one of

Essaouira's two Jewish cemeteries (the other, older one, containing a mausoleum of Rabbi Haïm Pinto, is across the road, being slowly ravaged by the Atlantic waves). Asher's grandfather, Rabbi David Knafo, was the chief rabbi and a rabbinical judge of Essaouira. He died in 1937 and was joined in the cemetery a few years later by two friends, Rabbi David Elkaïm and Rabbi David Yflah. As well as being a rabbi, David Elkaïm was a celebrated poet and stonemason.

Thanks to this unique combination of skills, the epitaphs of Mogador carved in the late nineteenth and early twentieth centuries have a rich poetry. Asher told me, "Elkaïm had many local imitators, and although he never signed his works, his monumental engravings are recognizable to those who know what to look for."

Through Asher, I met Haïm Bitton, then living between Morocco and San Diego, USA, as he lovingly restored Slat Lkahal. This historic building was one of some forty synagogues from the period when around half of Mogador's population was Jewish. An amateur historian, Haïm helped me piece together the rich Jewish heritage of Essaouira, which had begun when Sultan Sidi Mohammed Ben Abdullah invited prominent Jewish merchant families (many of whose ancestors had been expelled from Andalusia during the Reconquest) to settle in Mogador starting in the mid-eighteenth century. The Sultan had sought to orient his kingdom — and its trading links — toward the West, where he was the first foreign head of state to recognize US independence from Britain.

Even before the development of trade routes to Europe, Mogador was known as the port of Timbuktu, as it was located at the end of long caravan routes that brought goods and people and their traditions into North Africa and out across the Atlantic and into the Mediterranean. Haïm explained that Mogador had many British connections. He showed me an old tea chest in the synagogue dating from 1858. There are many theories regarding the origin of the Moroccan tradition of green tea with mint, but he was sure British traders were involved somehow, perhaps via networks of Jewish merchants between Mogador and Manchester. Another British link was Prime Minister Neville Chamberlain's war secretary during World War II, Leslie Hore Belisha, whose father had lived in the Mogador mellah (Jewish quarter).

Getting to Know the Locals

Living in Morocco, where the average standard of living is lower than in Europe, I was confronted on a daily basis with extreme poverty. That said, I still had much to be grateful for. Elhamdulillah.

I learned other "Allah phrases" to respond to requests for money as I moved around the medina.

Lah ysahel âalik means something like "may God make things easier for you."

Lah yster means something akin to "God protect you."

I often found myself explaining to foreign visitors that the lack of state-sponsored social safety net in Morocco was typically compensated by family and neighbors helping each other out. This meant that anyone encountered living on the street really had no one to support them. In such a community-focused society, this level of social isolation and vulnerability was shocking to me.

It was also through my work with the High Atlas Foundation that I got to know Association Bayti. Bayti means "my house," and the association is a national charity working with children from complex and challenging socioeconomic and family situations. Hassan is the indefatigable coordinator of the Bayti Centre in Essaouira. He graduated in sociology from Mohammed V University in Rabat, in a period when the makhzen (ruling elite) were restricting access to classes in the humanities and social sciences, as these subjects were deemed to have spawned too many left-leaning anti-regime activists.

Hassan's sense of social justice was born of the infamous Years of Lead, the 1960s to the 1980s, when the state suppressed opposition mercilessly, and it frames his work to this day.

Through Hassan, I learned of the children who couldn't be educated because their mothers feared repercussions for registering a birth outside of marriage. Without official identity papers, these children simply didn't exist in the eyes of the state.

I learned of a child forced to listen while his blind mother "paid her rent" for the shelter of an unsanitary slum of dubious ownership in the mellah, to a man pretending to be the landlord, in the only way a woman of no financial means could.

I also learned of the children who sell tissues to tourists, to bring in a family income instead of attending school.

At Bayti, children such as these receive social work support, a daily hot meal, and a place safe from the chaos at home to do their homework and realize their dreams. Those excluded from education follow a curriculum that makes it possible for them to join a mainstream school when their lives are stable.

While I was living in Essaouira, a record number of Bayti kids achieved their high school degree, enabling them to go on to university. Many of them were provided with school equipment through funds I raised alongside other local non-Moroccan residents.

The nearest university to Essaouira is in Marrakesh, and many students are daunted by the idea of living in a big city, or they simply can't afford it. This means they don't attend lectures consistently. Strong family ties, an obligation to bring income into the family, and the limited prospects of graduate-level employment mean that many young Moroccans consider university study a waste of time. All of these are reasons enrollment at Moroccan universities drops off sharply after the first year, when the state student grant falls away.

When I moved to Morocco in September 2012, Morocco's experience of the so-called Arab Spring was over. However, a number of graduates had taken the opportunity of that region-wide moment of protest to revive the activist spirit of the *diplomés chômeurs* (unemployed graduates) that had emerged during the period of political unrest of Hassan's student days in the 1990s.

Many days working for the High Atlas Foundation consisted of me scuttling from one *délégation* (local outposts of national ministries) to another, across the large paved square set back from the beach, seeking information, funds, and support for the Foundation's projects I managed. As I did, I saw groups of men and women staging demonstrations outside the provincial government building and the higher education *délégation*. Sometimes they waved banners; occasionally they banged pots; typically they had a tagine steaming on a makeshift brazier.

One day, my partner showed me a social media post by one of his friends who had been the victim of state brutality during one of these protests. He ended up in the hospital. I later interviewed him as part of the research for my master's dissertation, an ethnographic study of Essaouira's unemployed graduate protests during the Arab Spring.

By the time I was interviewing them, typically over many cups of hot, sweet mint tea in cafés around Essaouira after the nighttime tarawih prayers of Ramadan in 2018, most of the former *diplomés chômeurs* had succeeded in getting their stated goal of public sector employment. However, in a twist of their fate in a neoliberal globalized economy, new teaching jobs had become contractual and no longer offered the stability that the government jobs of the past had promised.

Many of the protesters — particularly the women — had hidden their participation from their friends and family, fearing criticism or shame. Several of my interviewees had never spoken of their participation to an outsider. Many expressed gratitude that I wanted to learn of their lived experiences and help them process what had been a stressful period in their lives, when they had chosen to throw their time and energy into protest at the risk of missing alternative employment opportunities and risking criticism or worse. They felt betrayed because the postcolonial promise that education would unlock access to the middle classes via stable government jobs had been whisked away from their generation, as the neoliberal state shrank, and everyone was encouraged to fend for themselves.

For young Moroccans – whether graduates or not — the lack of job opportunities is not only a financial concern, but it also delays their entry into true adulthood. For many young (and not-so-young) Swiris (as natives of Essaouira are called), it is not affordable to move out of the family home until they find stable employment. Furthermore, until they can do either of those things, they feel unable to get married and start a family of their own — both of which are culturally very important in Morocco. One local woman interviewed for my research told me that she wasn't married "because of unemployment." Now in her forties, she lamented, marriage offers came from unsuitably young men.

The lack of economic prospects impacts social mobility and explains why so many locals hope to find happiness in a partnership with a non-Moroccan. In a town like Essaouira, which is so dependent on tourism, the constant supply of unskilled labor from the surrounding area (Essaouira is one of Morocco's most rural provinces) keeps wages low and employment precarious. In this setting, where locals come into frequent contact with people from other countries and cultures, it is only natural that they dream of a worry-free life on the northern side of the Mediterranean. In the wake of COVID-19, which has decimated world tourism and had a knock-on effect on Essaouira's other main industry, fishing, as restaurants closed, it is hard to imagine sometimes the incredibly basic necessities Swiris dream of as I write this.

Living a Dream

Although not originally our plan (I never did open a bed-and-breakfast), departure from Morocco also became a shared dream for my partner and me. We are more fortunate than many Moroccans in that we had that choice.

In 2014, my partner became my husband. We were unceremoniously married in a small garage across the street from Essaouira's bus station. The courthouse, where the adoul (public notary) normally had his office, had been torn down to be rebuilt, and the temporary court accommodation was insufficient for notaries' offices. It was in this terribly unromantic setting that — with a leap of faith — we each signed our names on blank pieces of paper, above which our vows would be printed in Arabic, and my betrothed offered me a symbolic gift of two hundred Moroccan dirhams (about twenty dollars), which he had borrowed from a friend.

My in-laws threw a party at their home for our wedding. Our invitees were treated to "my" menu (seafood bastilla, a kind of phyllo pastry pie of seafood and noodles, because I don't eat meat) *and* the traditional beef and apricot tagine. After all the food and plenty of dancing, everyone slept well that night!

Feeling that our own social and economic opportunities were greater in my home country of Scotland, we left Morocco in December 2014, following a tortuous UK visa process. Our son, Rayyan, was born in Scotland in August 2015. Our small Scottish-Moroccan family lives a simple life, principally now in Edinburgh, blending what we can of our cultures, our traditions, and our languages, thereby creating something that is uniquely ours, *elhamdulillah*.

This story, however, is not only ours; it is the story of all those people who touched our shared lives over the last nine years, not just those I have mentioned here. I am grateful that our lives have intersected with theirs and for the chance to release their stories as well as mine.

Morocco is a nation of storytellers, but not every story has a voice. If I have been able to offer a voice to someone through my work and my writing, then all I can say is *elhamdulillah*.

A Biased Typographical Collection of Tangier
by Dina Benbrahim

The shapes of letters, their typography, often go unnoticed, yet they carry meaning — from the most functional to the most abstract. Words — and the shapes that form them — are loaded with emotion, associations, and stories. I first became a copywriter to play with how these words sound; then, as I grew as a designer, I experimented with their shapes and colors.

A lot of my fascination with typography probably has to do with where I grew up: Tangier. Yes, I grew up in Tangier, but I also grew up in my own little bubble. In this bubble, I was always daydreaming or chatting with imaginary friends. And in that bubble, the words that surrounded my daily life nourished my imagination. First, these words existed as the sounds that made them, and then they became words with shapes and colors.

Because Morocco is at the crossroads of several cultures, past and present, the poetry of words here is even more complex. These words have surrounded me in multiple languages since I was three apples tall — the sounds and accompanying shapes of Arabic, English, French, German, Italian, Spanish, Riffi, Tamazight, and others were all at play in my bubble.

What follows is a biased typographical collection of words with stories, all happening in my little bubble in Tangier, the Pearl of Morocco.

Amigo Restaurant

Question: Who is friends with soggy fries?

Answer: My brother. Me. And everyone else who grew up eating Amigo's creative bocadillos (sandwiches).

Amigo is a small restaurant. It has kept the same modest entrance and glass windows since it first opened its doors in 1969. The original Amigo' logotype was humble, hand-lettered in both Latin and Arabic characters on a white background. It was as if no real visual identity was needed because Tangier loved the mythic bocadillo by Amigo. It was anti-typography, if there is such a thing.

Everything at Amigo is handcrafted and has soul.

My older brother grabs my hand, and we go through the entire selection of mouthwatering ingredients behind the glass display. His treat. I start picking meats and tomatoes, peppers and pickles, onions and sauces to layer in a sandwich larger than one of my arms. Fries saturated with grease seal every Amigo sandwich. This sandwich is no exception.

Fries?

Yes, please. And don't skimp on the salt.

I could never finish my bocadillo. It was too big. A sandwich fit more for a basketball team than for just the little girl I was. But this sandwich of gargantuan proportions was more about having a moment between my brother and me than anything else.

Though Amigo is still around today, they have replaced that original hand-lettered placard — a disastrous type crime if there ever was one — but you can still share a moment with someone you love over the most delicious bocadillo that this side of the Strait of Gibraltar has to offer.

Gran Teatro Cervantes

Built in 1913 by Esperanza Orellana, Manuel Peña, and Antonio Gallego, this now-abandoned theater continues to fascinate me. The road leading to the theater is hilly, bumpy, and quite dark, even in midday. The wooden planks blocking its windows excite my curiosity. Nearby is an old shopping mall, a favorite of my mother and sister. While they perused the latest imported fashions, I would stick around just to admire the grandiose blue characters and multicolored ornaments of Gran Teatro Cervantes 1913.

Whereas sifting through piles of clothes, trying to find the newest, trendiest, most fashionable thing to wear drained me, typography lifted my mood even before I knew what typography was.

The font of the Teatro Cervantes' noticeably follows the aesthetic of the Arts and Crafts movement. This movement advocated for a keen attention to detail and refined hand-craftsmanship in opposition to the perceived dehumanizing industrialization.

The Cervantes' sign is certainly an iconic historical piece in which the craft is flawless. And in the midst of listening to stupid fights and unending negotiations for meaningless jeans, this sign can be a much-needed voyage into a happy place with sexy details.

Coloma Ice Cream

While I was growing up, our family's loud talks were sponsored by Coloma's ice cream shop. On weekends, I would always go with whichever of my parents or siblings was in charge of grabbing five big pots of ice cream and a stack of cones. From where I'm writing now, I can smell the candied scent of Coloma ice cream wafting up the bustling avenue from the sticky-sweet pots of the tiny, unassuming red-and-white store, as Proust smelled his madeleines.

Loud crowds pile up outside the modest white metallic door. A silence settles in my mind. I glance down, observing how all of the flavors and prices are delicately handwritten in Latin and Arabic letterforms — chalk on a blackboard. Cones and pot sizes are drawn like pictograms. The blackboard is full of life, pride, and humanity.

Minutes later, we are all crammed in the living room. It is almost midnight. Mom has her two lemon scoops, as always. The rest of us make a collective mess mixing tutti frutti, pistachio, chocolate and nata into individual cones.

I glance up at the light and close my eyes. I can feel its warmth radiating down. It's only been moments, but I feel the ice cream starting to drip down the side of the cone, spilling its syrupy deliciousness over my hand. Mom, dad, and my sisters all talk louder and louder while we slurp our melting mountains.

The conversation has turned political. Even in our family, we have conservatives and liberals, left and right wings of the same bird. And suddenly I know it's not only the light that's heating up; the conversation is as well. This is what happens when you discuss politics on a Coloma sugar rush!

I smile at the memory.

And to think, this little stroll down memory lane started as I pondered Coloma's blackboard in silence, from thousands of miles away.

Fondouq Chajra

I was one of those kids who loved to hang out in the maze of Fondouq Chajra, a local weaver's market of over fifty work spaces lining the edge of the old medina. While my parents were grocery shopping, my eyes wondered over the colorful textiles with their textures and red and blue stripes, and then, at the end of the market, I would find myself captivated by the little stores that seemed to me to sell every single product under the sun. Cans of sardines, bags of chips, cartons of milk, delicately packaged tissues, fingernail clippers, batteries of all sizes and shapes, a rainbow of lighters, glass jars of marmalade imported from France, diapers, guitar picks, dolls, puzzles, books and all of this and more piled up one on top of the other until they formed peaks reaching the corrugated metal ceiling. I had no interest in what they all contained (except for maybe the cereal boxes with their promise of a secret toy).

I was mostly captivated by the organization of multiple languages, textures, and styles to structure information on a single package. I also used to compare how vendors organized their stores. Starting from the cereal boxes with weird toys, I would observe what was in the foreground, what was kept in the background, and what was in between.

I grasped early on the efficiency of putting sweets at the nearest point from customers, and I discovered later that this retail merchandising strategy is universal.

Librairie des Colonnes

Until I was eighteen years old, all my books came from one tiny bookstore tucked in the folds of Boulevard Pasteur: Librairie des Colonnes. This particular bookstore, despite its Pompeian red façade with four vertical columns, is somehow unassuming. Even on the main street of Tangier, if you're not looking for it, it is small enough and easy to miss.

The Librairie des Colonnes has long kept a wide selection of classics in multiple languages. Its shelves are made of cedar. Every book you pick up carries the thick, homey scent of this wood, once taken from the faraway Middle Atlas mountains and lovingly planked all around the tiny bookstore.

I have spent countless hours inside and outside. Actually, now that I'm thinking about it, I probably could count exactly how many hours I've spent wrapped in the thick cedar smell, head bent over some classic, begging my mom to let me get this book this week so I might finish reading it at home — or passing it en route to my school just down the street, taking in the storefront as we slowly passed by. Let's see…

My parents drove my siblings and me by the bookstore five days a week, twice a day, to and from school. This means I spent approximately four thousand, six hundred and eighty minutes of my life looking at the Futura font of its façade.

Librairie des Colonnes was my very first encounter with this overused typeface, without being aware of it. As I grew up and noticed Futura applied on more store signs, Nike T-shirts, Volkswagen ads, and pretty much everything in between, I named it the Librairie des Colonnes text. I had a lot of fun spotting this font in my everyday life and, surprisingly, it never became a boring game.

For me, Futura will be forever mingled with the sounds of the bustling boulevard and the must of cedar wood.

Café Hafa

Café Hafa has overlooked the Strait of Gibraltar since 1921. It has proudly hosted the Beatles, the Rolling Stones, and others who have all come for a sip of their special mint tea.

From the outside is visible a hand-sculpted sign, in French and Arabic, with funky illustrations. The French letterforms alternate between capital letters and lowercase, and everything is painted in gold.

From the inside, a wall with analog typography showcases CAFE HAFA FONDE 1921, written with stones set into the cement wall. These stones have different thicknesses and sizes, making every letterform unique. I wonder if using stones was a secret welcome to all the stoners. Welcome to the magical world of Café Hafa, where you can get very stoned and it would be very OK.

From a design standpoint, the multiple inconsistencies by an untrained human hand make both signs cuter than cats on the Internet.

My mother volunteers at the orphanage La Crèche de Tanger, and I used to go with her quite often. We would drive by Café Hafa, and I would drool at the signs. I never dared to ask her to stop because I'd been raised to know that it was frowned upon for a girl to be seen at a coffee shop. When I bought my first camera as a young adult, I finally stopped by and captured these signs. By then, I was a rebel already. It did not matter to add one more frown to my list of frowns.

Ciné Roxy

I went to school a block from the Ciné Roxy, the neighborhood movie theater. The historic metallic sign on top of the building has been there since 1895. The serif and decorative letterforms sit on two baselines, and a third one is added to proudly hold a star, like the Star of Bethlehem. The hierarchy between the elements is wonderfully balanced.

When I was a teenager, I used to come to the cinema nearly every weekend to see Moroccan films or the latest imports from Spain, France, and the US. My best friend and I would watch the movies no one else cared about. People could still smoke in the theaters back in the nineties in Morocco. Around us, curls of blue and gray smoke filled the dark theater dramatically, blurring the couples making out, using the theater as their excuse for a romantic tryst. The seats were narrow and had an assortment of holes — cigarette burns, most likely — yet the ceiling was covered in gold paint.

The Art Deco theater — never full, only ever with a handful of couples kissing and smoking while we watched the movies — had such an underground yet majestic atmosphere. I cherished these moments. It was liberating to experience a lighter environment onscreen amidst so much darkness.

I have to add that I associate Roxy with the bakery next door. It has the greatest *petits pains à la crème* you have ever had, especially after inhaling so much secondhand smoke.

The theater has since been remodeled, you can no longer smoke there, and couples are carefully monitored, so kissing is much less frequent… but luckily the gorgeous letterforms, the romance, and the petits pains have survived.

Perdicaris Park

On sunny days, my parents and I would walk in the Perdicaris Park — a forested park on the outskirts of Tangier, atop the "big mountain" to the west — to admire the views of the sea from the top of the mountain and the fresh eucalyptus-scented air. At the end of the short hike, freshly squeezed orange juices waited for us.

Ion Perdicaris, a moneyed expat who had resided in Tangier, built a villa and a couple of smaller structures in early 1900s. He abandoned his property in Morocco in the 1930s, and right after the independence of 1956, his land became the Perdicaris Public Park.

During these hikes, I would wander in the abandoned structures, filled with handwritten words of love, names, and other graffiti. It was forbidden to write on the walls of our house. My dad gave a harsh lesson to my sister about it. However, everybody immortalized their stories with handwriting on Perdicaris' wall.

On one of these walls, I doodled my name, timidly and quickly. For the first time in my life I graffitied! I ran away bursting with joy. I had added my own sort of shape and color to the word that defined me: my name.

This was the start of long doodling sessions with chalk, brush pens, and gouache on the plywood inside my closet. I would climb up, curve my back, and fit my tiny body between the shelves. I would hide there for hours, building my non-prehistoric visual stories. I probably developed my beautiful scoliosis thanks to my creative posture, as I would stay in the zone like this until someone screamed my name to slurp up a soup. No wonder why I still hate soup!

* * *

Tangier's typography is timeless, and its timelessness extends to the entire country. The intricacy, intimacy, and, sometimes the simple functionality of it carries the imprint of multiple cultures coexisting across history and geography. It deserves to be noticed and talked, written, and dreamed about.

Hopefully, my warm memories are the start of another collection of stories about words with shape and soul — your stories.

A Night with the Nomads

by Alice Morrison

We were all nomads once. From our earliest emergence from the slime, through our evolution to all fours, then crouching, then standing tall, we moved forward relentlessly, our bodies evolving to help us cover the ground more easily. We hunted and gathered and sought shelter where we could find it, with only the most basic possessions and provisions. Women gave birth on the road, children grew up and grew strong or faded like daisies, and always we moved on.

Then we discovered agriculture and began to settle.

Families became villages, and villages became cities. Animals were no longer merely to be hunted; they were to be tamed and brought to shelter with us. People started to live longer and softer, and millennia by millennia we crept toward our present day, in which we move less than we sit, cover half the distance of the world for a holiday, and hate the thought of killing, even though we eat meat voraciously.

Some, though, still live in the older ways, moving with the seasons and living close to the land.

The Amazigh nomads of Morocco are seminomadic. Every year, they migrate from their winter home in the Jebel Saghro, the Mountain of Drought, to their summer pastures in Aït Bouguemez, Paradise Valley, where they can fatten up their flocks of goats and sheep on the green grass of this fertile area.

In May 2019, I joined Addi Bin Youssef and his family for a week as they migrated.

I knew Addi from a previous trip; he had been one of my companions on my four-thousand-kilometer expedition walking the whole of Morocco. I had spent three months with Addi, hearing about his family, his father's goats. "We have three hundred!" he'd tell me at regular intervals, and then ask me indecipherable nomad riddles. "Zahra," — my Moroccan name — "what has three eyes but cannot see, and one leg but cannot walk? And if you disobey me, you will surely be punished!"

"A traffic light," Addi eventually answered himself. "That's the answer to the riddle."

"Of course," I said.

Our months passed by like this. Addi peppered stories of family and his father's goats with these riddles.

When I joined him again in 2019, the migration for Addi and his family fell during Ramadan, which meant everyone was walking and moving their herds without being able to eat or drink between the hours of sunrise and sunset, roughly five in the morning to eight in the evening. I was fasting as well, and I was a bit nervous as to how I would manage the hills without any water, but I was also really excited to see what it would be like.

The trip was organized by Jean-Pierre from Dar Daïf in Ouarzazate; he was bringing along a group of European tourists. This is one way for nomads to earn supplementary income, and they are very happy to have guests around. For me, there was an added bonus: two of my other companions from the Morocco crossing, Brahim Ahalfi and Brahim Boutkhoum, would also be traveling to look after the guests. This meant I could spend time with them, and also celebrate Ramadan with them.

*   *   *

I arrived a day early so that I could get to know Addi's family before we set off. They were camped on a hill above a dry river valley. Addi came bounding down as we drove up. I hadn't seen him for two months. He was taller than I remembered and, somehow, even more of an adult.

"Zahra!" he yelled. "Salaam alykum!"

He took me up to his family home, a spacious goat-hair tent, held up by central poles fixed into a large stone block and tied down at the edges but with the sides open and with bright handmade rugs covering the floor. There I was proudly introduced to his mother, Ito; his sister, Aicha; and his sister-in-law, Fatima. All of the women were small and slight. Fatima had a baby strapped to her back and her three-year-old, Hannan, buzzing around her like a bee on speed. Ito had delicate tattoos on her face, an old Amazigh custom.

Language was a potential barrier, because although I have begun to learn Tamazight (or, more specifically, Tachelhit), I still only speak a little, and the women spoke no Arabic. I had two good weapons in my armory, though: lots of pictures of Addi on my phone from the expedition and a one large packet of henna.

I asked Ito to help me henna my feet and hands, to ready for the trip ahead. She mixed up the henna powder with water and a little oil into a thick green paste and then smeared it onto my hands and feet, and tied plastic around them so that the henna could settle. There was nothing to do now but wait for the three hours that it takes for the paste to work.

It was midday, so we all settled down for a nap. You have to be comfortable with silence and fitting in, so I lay down and let the time pass, watching the baby goats chase each other around the tent poles. One mother goat had come to sleep next to Addi's uncle, who was stretched out next to me. The wind was quite strong on the top of the hill, and if it gusted too hard, one of the women would leap up and grab hold of the tent pole.

I was having a struggle of my own. I was dressed very modestly in leggings and a caftan, but we were all sardined in, and because I was lying on a slope, I kept slipping down, and my caftan kept riding up. My leggings had left a little strip of leg exposed to the sun, which duly burnt the strip a dull red. I could neither pull my caftan down nor my leggings up because my hands were tied into plastic bags, and everyone was snoozing around me. The embarrassment of my hoisted caftan was worse than the sunburn.

About two hours before sundown, the women started working for the evening meal. I had been liberated from my bags, and my feet and hands were a gratifying orange color from the dye. Henna is a skin strengthener and a disinfectant, which helps when you are doing lots of physical traveling. I was dispatched by

Ito to bring back wood, and I went off up the hill grateful for something to do.

"Good," she smiled at me when I got back, although she was probably just being nice, because her bundle was much bigger. Meanwhile, Aicha had been kneading the bread, and it was sitting under a cloth, proofing until ready to bake when the fire was set. She had also started the soup, which is a vital ingredient for Ramadan.

I wasn't sure exactly where I should be. Should I be eating with the Brahims and the other cameleers who had come to help the western guests? Or should I be with the family?

Addi soon put me right. "You'll have break-fast with us, Zahra," he told me firmly.

That was easily settled. I would break the fast with the family.

Behind our tent, the men were laying out the rugs facing in the direction of Mecca, ready for the sunset prayer. As the sun disappeared over the hills, Brahim's voice rang out with the call, and that was our signal for dates and water. That first sip is so good and sweet and brings instant relief after a day of thirst. The dates, too, are a sugar rush of goodness.

I wasn't absolutely clear about what to do next, so I watched carefully and tried not to make any socially awkward mistakes. The men prayed and the women got the soup and dates and bread ready. Then we all sat in a circle and ate together. I was painfully aware of how precious food is, and that there wasn't an endless supply of it, so I didn't eat too much. As a treat, we also had some eggs.

After the meal, everyone sat and chatted, and Brahim came up from the other tents to join us. I couldn't understand much of what was being said around me, but I could hear that the talk was about what the goats would fetch at market and some discussion of the visitors who would arrive tomorrow.

I was so happy to be sitting there with Addi and his family, seeing him in his own domain, being treated like a king by his mum. She obviously adored him, and they were joking and giggling under one of the blankets that we had all drawn up to combat the cold. Ito tried on my woolly hat, perching it on top of her head and laughing hysterically at the picture I took. Hannan and the baby had been put to sleep under the blankets.

"Watch out, Zahra!" yelled Fatima as I almost sat on them, not realizing what the lumps were.

Then Aicha, who had disappeared for ages, reappeared with a big pot of tagine. One of the benefits for the nomads of having tourists with them for their weeklong migration is that they get more provisions than usual. Addi went round with a kettle of water and poured it over our hands so that we could wash them and handed me a little towel to dry them. I didn't know if the men and women would eat separately, but I was pulled into the circle, tucked up in a blanket and handed some smoky, crisp-on-the-outside bread.

"In the name of God," we said and dipped our bread into the sauce and then worked up to the vegetables. Ito gathered all the meat into a pile and then divided it exactly so that we all got a fair share of protein.

The conversation flowed around me. Occasionally I was asked something by Addi, but for most of the time I sat quietly, enjoying being in a family and the feeling of human companionship, and the light of the stars, shining so clearly above us.

When I think of Morocco, this is what I think of. I think of Addi and Ito and their family and that night in Jebel Saghro under the stars, with the nomads, preparing for the annual migration. I think of the companionship, the quiet anticipation, and I remember our bellies, full and warm.

Tales Told to a Melon

by Tahir Shah

Known to his friends as the Melon King, Yahya had a mischievous glint in his eye and the most infectious smile. He'd been born on a rocky scrap of land overlooking the Atlantic shore, back in the days when King Mohammed V was on the throne. On his head he wore a tattered old hat he'd woven himself from straw, and on his feet were yellow babouches, their leather as coarse and worn as his palms. The first words he ever spoke in my direction were these:

"You've not lived until you have known the life of a melon."

We were sitting on the porch of his shack, close to Dar Khalifa, where I lived. As the golden summer sun eased low toward the waves, I turned the words over in my mind.

Yahya grinned, his eyes glinting fiery red.

"I'll tell you a secret," he said.

I leaned in so as to hear all the better.

"Given a chance, a melon will teach you, and it will feed you as well."

"That's the secret?"

Yahya nodded, the side of his face lost in shadow.

I asked what he meant.

He didn't answer, not at first. But then, as the orange orb dipped below the horizon, he said,

"Some things cannot be explained. They must be experienced."

Again, I probed what he meant.

The Melon King took out a handkerchief, dabbed it roughly over his face, peered down at the shore, and turned to me.

"I have a gift for you," he said.

"Thank you, but there's really no need."

Stuffing away the cloth, Yahya nudged a thumb and forefinger beneath the band of his tattered old hat, foraged about, and tapped something onto the tabletop.

A black seed. A watermelon seed.

"For you."

Wondering what exactly I was supposed to do, I gave thanks.

"Should I peel it before eating?" I asked.

Yahya stared across at me in shock.

"No!"

"Not peel?"

"No, no, no… The seed's not for eating, not until it's grown into a delicious fruit."

"Then what should I do with it…with my gift?"

"You must plant it," the Melon King explained.

"Where?"

"In the garden courtyard at your home."

* * *

An hour or so later I was back at Dar Khalifa, the mansion I'd bought four years previously, located slap-bang in the middle of a Casablanca shantytown.

My children, Ariane and Timur, found me in the sitting room when they came home from school.

"What's wrong, Baba?" Ariane asked.

I explained how Yahya, the Melon King, had entrusted a seed to me, along with a list of precise instructions.

Timur jerked a thumb at the seed then at the large courtyard garden outside my library.

"Let's get to it," he said.

Before I knew it, he and Ariane had fetched a trowel, a watering can, and a long bamboo cane. Having planted tomato seeds at school, they were instant experts. While I watched, they showed me how to embed the melon seed so that it would grow just right.

Once covered in half an inch of soil, they sprinkled it with water and marked the place with the cane.

"What do we do now?" I asked.

"We wait," Ariane said firmly.

Timur rolled his eyes.

"We'll die of boredom," he moaned.

"No, we won't!" Ariane shot back.

Running into the kitchen, she grabbed a blue magnet from the fridge – an evil eye averter –and set it squarely in front of where the seed was interred.

Days passed.

I got on with writing a book about the legacy of stories and storytelling in Morocco. A writer on a deadline shuts out the world, even if there are seeds to be coaxed into melons, and that's what happened.

Ten days after the planting ritual, the kids stomped in from school and hurried into my office, where I was fighting procrastination.

"It's growing!" they both yelled at once.

"What is?"

"The melon seed!"

We hurried out into the courtyard garden. Following the line of Timur's index finger, I spotted a good-size shoot. Fresh green, it was seemingly curious, as though new to the world.

Over the weeks, the three of us tended to the sapling as it developed into a pleasing little plant, with a single pea-like fruit. Each couple of days we'd sprinkle it with filtered water, shade it from the dazzling summer light, and protect it from the rats, which swarmed in over the walls at night from the shantytown.

As the little sapling grew, I found myself reflecting on Yahya, the Melon King, and on my own unlikely connection with the fruit.

You see, melons, or rather, stories connected to melons, have been in my head for as long as I can remember.

*   *   *

It all began when, on my fifth birthday, my father gave me an exquisite box.

Crafted from turquoise micro-mosaic, it was adorned along the edges with ivory beading. It was about twelve inches long and half as wide.

My father said it came from Paghman, the ancestral home of our family in Afghanistan, and had been passed down through generations. I was used to being given boring wooden blocks and cheap plastic toys, and so the box caught my attention. It was the sort of thing that is sometimes kept away from children because of its delicacy and value.

I laid it on my bed and carefully removed the lid.

Inside were three orderly sheets of paper, all folded up.

Pulling out the pages, I looked at the lines of type and asked what all the writing meant. My father sat on the edge of my bed and said that the writing was a story, a story as old as the world. He said it was very important and that I would learn to appreciate it, as if it were one of my friends.

I asked him about the box. I was so small, but I remember his exact words.

"This box is very lovely," he said. "You can see the colors and the work on the sides. But don't be fooled, Tahir Jan, the box is only a container. What's held inside is far, far more precious. One day you'll understand."

As usual I didn't see what he meant, and didn't know what he was talking about.

To my eyes, the box was the box, and the story on the paper was a story, and no more than that. The gift was put on a high shelf in my bedroom and brought down to be admired from time to time. The pages inside stayed protected by the box but yellowed with time. They're still in there, in the very same box, which now sits in my library on my desk.

Sometimes when I feel the need, I open the box, take out the story, and read it.

It's "The Tale of Melon City"…

*   *   *

The Tale of Melon City

Once upon a time the ruler of a distant land decided to build a magnificent triumphal arch, so that he could ride under it endlessly with great pomp and ceremony.

He gave instructions for the arch's design, and work began.

The masons toiled day and night until the great arch was at last ready.

Then the king had a fabulous procession assembled of courtiers and royal guards, all dressed in their finest costumes.

Taking his position at the head, the procession moved forward. But as the king rode through the great arch, his royal crown was knocked off.

Infuriated, he ordered the master builder to be hanged.

A gallows was constructed in the main square, and the chief builder was led towards it. As he climbed the steps of the scaffold, he called out that the fault lay not with him, but rather with the men who'd heaved the blocks into place.

They, in turn, put the blame on the masons who had cut the blocks of stone.

The king had the masons dragged to the palace.

They were ordered to explain themselves on pain of death. The masons insisted the fault lay at the hands of the architect whose blueprint they'd followed.

The architect was summoned. He revealed to the court that he was not to blame, for he'd only followed the plans drawn up by the order of the king. Unsure who to execute, the king summoned the wisest of his advisers, who was very ancient indeed.

The situation was explained to him in detail.

Just before he was about to give his solution, he expired.

The chief judge was called. He decreed that the arch itself should be hanged. But because the upper portion had not touched the royal head, it was exempted. So a hangman's noose was brought to the lower portion, so that it could be punished on behalf of the entire arch.

The executioner tried to attach his noose to the arch, but realized it was far too short. The judge called the rope maker, but he stated it was the fault of the scaffold, not the rope, for being too short.

Presiding over the confusion, the king saw the impatience of the crowd.

"They want to hang someone," he said anxiously. "We must find someone who will fit the gallows."

Every man, woman, and child in the kingdom was measured by a special panel of experts. Even the king's height was measured. By a strange coincidence, the monarch himself was found to be the perfect height for the scaffold.

A victim secured, the crowd calmed down.

Without delay, the king was led up the steps, had the noose slipped round his neck, and was hanged.

According to the kingdom's custom, the next stranger who ventured through the city gates could decide who would be the new monarch. The courtiers ran to the city gate and waited for a stranger to arrive.

They waited and waited, and waited and waited.

Eventually they spotted a man in the distance.

He was riding a donkey backwards.

As soon as he passed through the great city gate, the prime minister scurried up and asked him to choose the next king.

The man, who was a traveling idiot, said, "A melon." He said this because he always said "a melon" to anything that was asked of him. For he liked to eat melons very much.

And so it came about that a melon was crowned king.

All these events happened long, long ago.

A melon is still king of the country, and when foreigners visit and ask anyone there why a melon's the ruler, they say it's because of tradition, that the king prefers to be a melon, and that they, as humble subjects, have no power to change his mind.

*   *   *

One afternoon, once we'd tended to the precious young melon, I told Ariane and Timur the story of Melon City, the tale I'd kept protected in a box since I was their age.

Ariane said the melon wasn't actually a melon at all, but that it was a time machine in disguise. Each night, she revealed, it turned back from a melon into itself and would crisscross time and space, seeking answers from the universe.

I asked how she had come by such information.

"The melon told me," she said.

* * *

As the melon grew, so did interest in it.

All of a sudden it seemed that everyone had an opinion on how to care for the fruit, which had now swelled to the size of a tennis ball.

Zohra, our housekeeper, flustered out of the kitchen and insisted that we tie scraps of red cloth to the leaves. She warned that if we failed to follow her advice, the melon would poison anyone who tasted it.

Next on the scene was Abdullah, the chief guardian.

He claimed a female jinni living under the courtyard garden had already laid claim to the melon. If the fruit wasn't presented to her on a bed of vine leaves, he said, the entire house was in danger of being turned into dust.

The next morning, there was a knock at Dar Khalifa's main door. The guardians were nowhere to be seen, so I ventured out to check who was there.

It was the Melon King.

"Everyone's talking about your melon," he said.

"Everyone?"

"Yes."

"Everyone who?"

"Everyone worth listening to."

I invited Yahya inside.

We made our way through the house and into the courtyard garden, where water, issuing from a magnificent mosaic fountain on the far wall, cooled the air.

As soon as the Melon King set eyes on the fruit, he grinned a Cheshire Cat grin.

"You've done well," he said.

"My children have been helping me," I said modestly.

"So you've all done well."

"Do you think we are watering it too much?" I asked.

Yahya touched a hand to the soil.

"Perfect."

"What about the sunlight? Are we giving it enough?"

"Plenty."

I sighed with relief.

As we stood there, both gazing at the little melon, Yahya winked.

"There's a secret to growing melons," he said.

"A secret that's made you the Melon King?"

"Yes."

"Is there any way that part of the secret could be passed on to novice melon growers like us?"

Yahya grinned all the wider.

"You must talk to your melons," he said.

"That's it? That's the secret?"

The Melon King nodded.

"What do you tell them?"

"Anything you like. You can read from the newspaper, or talk about your life and adventures, but there's something they like most of all."

"What?"

"Stories."

"What kind of stories?"

"Stories about melons."

"I've already told the story of Melon City," I said brightly.

"To the melon?"

"Well, kind of. I told it to my kids…and I'm pretty sure the melon heard."

"That's not the same thing. You must speak directly to the melon."

I scratched my head.

"But I don't know any other stories about melons."

"Then make them up," Yahya said.

So I did.

* * *

Over the next weeks I told the melon growing in the courtyard garden tales about melon kings and queens, melon warriors, melon explorers, and even one about a princess who was wedded to a dashing prince, then transformed into a melon by a wicked witch.

I couldn't say for sure whether the melon we'd reared from a seed was benefiting from all the attention. What was more certain was that day by day it continued to grow, until it was the size of a soccer ball.

Each afternoon, when the kids came in from school, we poured a full bucket of water over the ground on which the melon was growing.

Then, in what had become a kind of evening ritual, I recounted a new tale.

When my father died, I inherited his library, containing hundreds of books of stories collected from all corners of the world. After Yahya's visit I'd scoured them for tales of melons but had come up with only two or three. So in my desperation to keep the fruit happy, I wrote a manuscript entitled *Tales Told to a Melon*.

The stories I wrote on melons were inspired by oral folklore passed to me by Zohra, the guardians, the blacksmith, and a host of others who were on the payroll. As anyone who's ever renovated a sprawling mansion set squarely in the middle of a Casablanca shantytown knows, hiring people in Morocco is as easy as laying them off is challenging.

Little by little, the tales of melons sewed themselves together into a patchwork quilt of wonder – a quilt as much about Morocco and its ancient threads of life, as it was about pleasing a watermelon that was swelling by the day.

*   *   *

Many weeks after we had planted Yahya's seed, the melon was enormous.

Ariane brought the scales down from the bathroom. With some difficulty, we managed to slip them beneath it.

Triumphantly, Timur called out the weight: "Eleven and a half kilograms!"

"Do you think it's ready?" I asked.

"Ready for what, Baba?" Ariane asked.

"Ready to eat."

As soon as the words left my mouth, Ariane and Timur burst into tears.

"You can't eat Alexandra!" they bawled.

"Alexandra? Who's Alexandra?"

"The melon."

"But melons don't have names," I said.

"Our melon does," Timur replied pointedly. "We love her."

"She's our pet melon, and no one's ever going to kill her and eat her."

Lowering myself down on the step beneath the fountain, I coaxed the children to gather round. We sat in silence for a long time, listening to the water flowing, and staring at Alexandra. Striped green and white, her taut skin seemed to gleam in the yellow afternoon sunshine.

"Last night I had a dream," I said.

"A nice one?" Ariane asked.

"A very nice one."

"What was it?"

"I dreamt that Alexandra was the kindest, happiest melon in all the world."

"She is," Timur blurted.

"I know she is. And that's how I dreamt her being."

"I want to promise you both something."

"What, Baba?"

"That if we let Alexandra do what she's supposed to do – to refresh our friends in the shantytown – I'll make sure that no one ever forgets her."

"How'll you do that?"

Leading Ariane and Timur through the carved cedar doors into my library, I held up a wad of papers on my desk.

"Because of this," I said, holding up the manuscript of *Tales Told to a Melon*.

"What is it?"

"It's a little book I've written in honor of the cleverest, kindest, most beautiful melon that ever lived."

* * *

The next evening, we got dressed up in our best clothes and sent a message for Yahya to join us, along with Zohra, the blacksmith, the guardians, and all the others who'd squirmed their way onto Dar Khalifa's payroll.

Ariane and Timur had filled a little basket with pink and white rose petals they'd gathered from the garden. Standing beside their pet melon, they showered it in petals while singing a song they'd made up on the way home from school.

As we all clustered around, the Melon King said a blessing and gave thanks to the courtyard garden for nurturing such a magnificent fruit.

Then, pulling a penknife from his belt, Yahya clipped the melon free.

A moment later, it had been cleaved into slices, which were passed around. There was so much melon that a stream of people flooded in from the shantytown to quench their thirst on Alexandra.

Ariane and Timur had been reluctant to taste their pet. But, seeing mile-wide grins on all the faces, they gave in and feasted as well.

"Delicious," Timur said.

"Refreshing," Ariane added.

One by one, the visitors gave thanks and filed away into the night.

Yahya was the last to leave. The children and I walked him to the door, the air fragrant with datura flowers. Pausing, he gave sincere thanks, and said:

"Some people think melon seeds are worthless, but they're not. They're a reflection of Morocco. Give them the right conditions, love them as you've done… tell them stories and sing to them… and they'll return all you've given them a thousand times over."

Stooping down to their height, he presented Ariane and Timur with a little bag packed with damp melon seeds – seeds gathered from their beloved Alexandra.

"Plant some of these tomorrow," he said in no more than a whisper. "Before you know it, you'll have an entire field of melons."

"Can we give them all names?" Ariane asked.

"Of course you can."

"Can we keep them as pets?" Timur whispered.

"Yes."

"But what happens when our melons are eaten?"

Yahya, the Melon King, broke into laughter.

"Save the seeds, plant them, and the magic begins all over again."

Living in a Museum in Tangier

by Gerald Loftus

When people imagine an expat's life in Morocco, what do they see? Luxuriating on beaches or strolling through the souks of Marrakesh. Romantic notions of arabesque refurbished riads abound, designer-perfect and easily available through AirBnB. Heroic — and sometimes hilarious — accounts of battling with dubious building contractors (and supernatural jinn), as in Tahir Shah's delightful memoir *The Caliph's House*. But what is life like in America's only National Historic Landmark located abroad, living upstairs from the museum that is the Tangier American Legation? Let me tell you.

Tangier, where Americans first set foot just after the Revolutionary War, and where we looked out over the flat rooftops of the ancient medina to Spain, as the very modern tankers and container ships plied the Strait of Gibraltar.

That was the centerpiece of my Morocco — and that of my wife, Marie Hélène — in the four years that I was the director of TALIM, the Tangier American Legation Institute for Moroccan Studies, a nonprofit academic research center that doubles as a museum recounting the history of America's first diplomatic property. More on that fascinating history later. But other than *Night at the Museum*, few people can imagine what it is like to live in the place you work, especially when that place is a museum.

Like Ben Stiller's museum guard, we too had Teddy Roosevelt to keep us company...

President Theodore Roosevelt reacting to the kidnapping of American Ion Perdicaris by Moroccan chieftan Raisuli in Tangier in 1904. Illustration by Lawrence Mynott in *Lions at the Legation & Other Tales: Two Centuries of American Diplomatic Life in Tangier*, by Gerald Loftus

Here's the quandary about writing on my experience living in Morocco in the second decade of the twenty-first century:

though we certainly lived among contemporary Moroccans, Americans, and Europeans as friends, colleagues, and neighbors, I also felt surrounded, not by jinn or ghosts, but by the memory of those who had lived there in decades and centuries past.

So there it is: "my Morocco" is also the Morocco of the 1830s American Consuls who had to deal with successive sultans' gifts of Atlas lions destined for the President of the United States; of World War II skullduggery in the Rif mountains by secret agents of the pre-CIA Office of Strategic Services (OSS); and of the quasi hippie Peace Corps volunteers in training at the Legation in the seventies, who turned an underground (and dried-up) water reservoir into a disco they named "the Cistern Chapel." Living in the present — while imagining life there in the past — was a large part of the pleasure of my years in Tangier.

Sometimes the past came back, not to haunt us, but to wake us up in the middle of the night.

With its massive nineteenth-century iron-studded doors (actually, doors-withincarriage gates), entry after hours to the museum is only possible by getting the guards' attention to open the huge deadbolts.

We heard the commotion — banging, shouting, the latter sounding a bit infused with alcohol — and by the time I got dressed to go downstairs, the guard had already persuaded the "intruder" to go home. The intruder had simply wanted "the Consul" to intervene in some domestic dispute. Now, there hasn't been an American Consul at the Legation since 1961, but it gives you an idea of the lingering semiofficial aura of the place. Even today, utility bills are still addressed to "the American Consulate," almost six decades after it moved to modern premises (also long since closed) outside the medina.

Like many foreigners living in Morocco and, to be honest, home keepers in general, we have also had to deal with contractors galore. The building where the consulate stands was given to the United States in 1821 by the Sultan of Morocco. Because of its age, it needs constant refurbishment and repair, and historical restoration is rendered more complex when your landlord is the US Government and you are located across the Atlantic in a foreign country.

The American Legation is the first and oldest US diplomatic property. Care of the building is a balancing act between local Legation staff, the American Embassy and its contractors in the capital Rabat, and the historical preservation professionals at the State Department's Overseas Building Operations in Washington.

Oh, yes — about those contractors.

We were fortunate to have mostly good experiences, especially in the form of a Tangier-born entrepreneur, Carlos Hadad, whose knowledge of the building goes back decades. Carlos is a great example of "international Tangier," that mix of religions, nationalities, and cultures that flourished in the first part of the twentieth century, and that still shows in the vibrant mix of people who have made Tangier their home. Son of a Moroccan-Jewish father and a Spanish mother (Spaniards once comprised the majority of the European population of the city, and Spanish is widely spoken in shops and by Tangerinos in general), Carlos brings Moroccan sensibilities and European craftsmanship to his work keeping the Legation ticking.

Jinn — nothing as tragicomic as Tahir Shah's nighttime encounters in *The Caliph's House*, but we did experience a series of mini-disasters we called "The Day of the Jinn."

On the eve of our departure on an international trip, when all we wanted was to pack and finish last-minute tasks, we had, in rapid order:

(1) a spontaneous explosion of the glass window on our oven;

(2) a false alarm over what I thought was the key falling into a locked file cabinet;

(3) water running down the wall behind our bed, the accumulation of a waterlogged wall finally overflowing.

As I say, nothing so dramatic that it couldn't be handled by Carlos, but it did get us wondering about those old tales they used to tell about jinn "haunting" the Legation building (probably designed to scare neighborhood kids away, which — coupled with the imposing Marine guards that used to be posted outside in its days as a diplomatic compound — would be pretty formidable dissuasion).

When I arrived in summer 2010 to take up my new job, I could choose where to set up my office in the sprawling Legation. First I had to navigate the five different staircases and fifty-some rooms, divided between museum space, offices, and living and guest quarters. I brought my own laptop and tablet, which meant I could work wherever was most convenient. I eventually settled on the research library, a particularly enchanting part of the Legation, replete with inner covered courtyard, arches, and a massive Moroccan stained-glass lantern. An office in a library, and an apartment in (actually, above) a museum — what more could I want?

As much as I loved the architecture, it was the book collection that was the real attraction. One of its most valuable features (to historians) is a beautiful leather-bound collection of the *Tangier Gazette*, a weekly newspaper in English, French, and Spanish editions, going back to the late nineteenth century. Though there were a few tantalizing gaps in the collection, it remains a valued resource for scholars looking for contemporary coverage of events in Morocco during such periods as the Spanish occupation of Tangier during the Second World War, or the unrest in the last days of freewheeling "International Zone" Tangier, eventually leading to Morocco's independence in 1956.

The *Tangier Gazette* also provided material for yours truly, an amateur museum curator and blogger in search of stories.

The TALIM Director's Blog became a vehicle to tell the many intriguing stories of encounters between Moroccans, Americans, and others in Tangier, Morocco's window on the outside world for centuries. And the library provided inspiration for exhibits in the museum, notably on the close to two hundred years (the Legation bicentennial year is 2021) since it became the home of generations of American diplomats.

To really appreciate how unique the Tangier American Legation is, you might start by running that phrase through a search engine. You'll learn that "legations" have all disappeared, replaced in the 1950s by embassies. All the Morocco tourist guidebooks, from Lonely Planet to the Guide du Routard, sing the praises of the Tangier American Legation museum, but you might need a good map to locate it, hidden as it is just inside the walled, mostly narrow pedestrian streets of the medina of Tangier.

Whatever you do, I hope you don't fall into the hands of the infamous faux guides (if you must hire a personal guide, make it an official one). I lost track of the times I would overhear a make-believe "guide" tell tourists crazy stuff outside the window, like "George Washington slept here," or useless information on the order of "the Legation has seven doors on this pedestrian street." What does that matter to the curious tourist if you then whisk them away so they can buy trinkets in your cousin's shop, without ever stepping inside the number one cultural tourism site in Tangier?

But when the persistent visitor found their way to this hidden gem, we wanted to make sure that they came away with an appreciation of how rare it is to walk through a living example of what diplomacy was like before video conferences and email. There is the 1865 original of the announcement by the Consul of the assassination of Abraham Lincoln, and an American flag rug woven by Moroccan women in gratitude for the US role in Morocco's independence. And a facsimile of an 1839 letter (the original is in the US National Archives) from the Consul to the Secretary of State, lamenting how he was burdened by the gift of lions destined for the President (an early test of the "Emoluments Clause" of the Constitution).

> himself, but before the letter could be prepared the sound of drums announced the arrival of the Bashaw's Nephew at the head of a troop of soldiers with an enormous, magnificent Lion & Lioness. As my determination was well known the commander of the troop had prepared himself with the most "conclusive answers" to all my objections. I told him that is was perfectly impossible to receive the animals, the Laws of my country forbid it. He replied that they were not—

Excerpt of letter from Consul Thomas Carr to the Secretary of State, September 3, 1839

There — see how easily I slipped down another nineteenth-century rabbit hole? That's the way it is at the Legation. But when we come up to the surface in the present-day Legation, there is plenty of good stuff to be found, too — like the dozens of women who show up every day for their Arabic literacy classes.

This program, which happens in the former consular offices (now all converted to classrooms), was begun more than twenty years ago in partnership with a Moroccan civic group, La Fondation Tanger Al-Madina (FTAM). The core program is teaching written Arabic to women whose schooling was either interrupted or never began. Many turn up after a day's work, and some bring along their young children.

Lesson One, Day One has not changed in these two decades: how to hold and use a pencil.

Fatima Benguerch is their teacher, herself from modest circumstances in the medina and the first in her family to graduate from university. Marie Hélène and other expat women taught French classes, and the women can also take cooking and sewing courses. A number of women learn skills that can lead to employment, and all of them enjoy the "safe space" among women to express themselves and expand their knowledge. It's a great program that anchors the Legation in what is an impoverished part of the city. When we return to Tangier to see friends, it's always so touching to have an elderly, veiled woman, passing on a busy street, reach out to embrace her former French teacher. Salt of the earth.

So that's "our Morocco," in a nutshell. Like many foreigners, we're smitten by the warmth and generosity of Moroccans and always feel at home when we return. But we have a few additional friends that no one else can see, and they're also there to keep us company.

There's Sidney Paley, the modern-day American pirate, tried at the Legation Consular Court in the early 1950s (he got a reduced sentence and said he'd go back to his original occupation — smuggling).

And then there's Dean of Dean's Bar, a wartime man of mystery who'd remind you of "Rick" and his café in *Casablanca*.

There's Raisuli, the bandit who kidnapped an American and was played by Sean Connery in *The Wind and the Lion*.

There's ... you know I could go on forever. "My Morocco" is in the present, and of the past. A bit of real-time traveling, thanks to living in a museum.

Couscous Friday

by Myronn Hardy

A handful of couscous is better than Mecca and all its dust.

— Moroccan proverb

I buy pastries: almond-stuffed kaab el ghazal, sesame-sprinkled, honey-drenched chebekia, and lemon tarts. I watch the woman at the counter carefully place the pastries in a white box, cut a silver ribbon, and tie it about. She pushes the box toward me to take. I check my watch. I'm on time. I leave the café-bakery to walk from downtown to the city's center, near the market, toward a hill where sandstone is exposed — the sandstone where, secretly, young and not-so-young artists have carved a horse, a giant sycamore leaf, an acorn. I lean against the rusty bars of the wrought-iron gate nearby.

I'm waiting for the most important Friday prayer to end. I'm waiting for the mosque to open its doors to let out its faithful practitioners. I'm waiting for Salim. He invited me to have couscous at his family's home.

It is autumn and warm and the breeze through the oak branches is both pleasant and loud. I'm looking at my non-smart phone, reading messages I've previously read to seem involved in something other than waiting as cars pass, as the occasional person walks by.

I hear Salim from across the street. He's asking me if I've been waiting long. I tell him no.

"My mother is waiting for us," he says.

As we walk to his house, I tell him that my class begins in a little over an hour.

"We will be back in time," he says. "I do not have to be at work for an hour and a half."

I met Salim when he came to my office to set up my computer. He works in the Information Technology Department of the University where we're employed. During that office visit, he told me how he watches an American movie every evening. And that Denzel Washington is his favorite actor. He likes the postcard I have of the Brooklyn Bridge on the wall. I told him I love walking across the bridge, that that walk makes me believe in every New York City myth — they are all real. He also told me he assumed, when he saw me on campus, that I was a student, that I was Moroccan. Those assumptions made me consider that the distance I felt from everything wasn't what others, perhaps, felt from me. I was familiar, seemed familiar, close without knowing so.

Near his home, I walk with him to a small store. On its few shelves are boxed juices, bottled soda, soap, and a small basket of apples. He buys a sixty-four-ounce bottle of Coca-Cola and another of Sprite. He points to the box I'm holding in my hand.

"These are pastries for your mom," I say.

"You do not have to bring anything, Myronn." He rolls the "r" in my name. "My mother has made everything."

Salim pushes open the front door previously ajar. The sun hits the plastic-protected yellow-and-blue-upholstered sofas. He pulls off his shoes and I do the same. He walks to the kitchen and I remain in the living room. I place my backpack on the floor. Salim's mother emerges from the kitchen, a veil over her head. Salim's nose and pale brown eyes are the same as hers. He introduces us. I hand her the box of pastries. She takes them and asks, "Why?"

"You invited me," I say and Salim translates.

"He is kind. Is he Muslim?" she asks Salim. He looks at me without translating. But even though I'd been in the country for a very short time, I'd encountered that question often. I hear the surprise, feel it when the one asking discovers I'm not Muslim. I'm the unfathomable, a kind non-Muslim. The exception to what many are taught, hear all of their lives.

She stretches her right arm for me to sit. Both she and Salim return to the kitchen. The front door isn't closed, and a man, older, in his late sixties or early seventies, walks inside. "Salaam," he says. I smile, repeating the word. Salim comes from the kitchen and introduces us.

"This is the neighbor," he says.

"Nice to meet you," I say.

"Americani?" he asks Salim.

"Yes," I say, "New York City."

His clothes are khaki: pants, shirt, belt. His full head of hair is silvery-white. He sits on the other side of the sofa to face me.

"Obama," he says. I hesitantly nod. I look at the space of the open door: the gravel and weeds interspersing, the finches darting, some of them landing on the ground to chirp then fly elsewhere, a green Peugeot at the bottom of the hill. A child, who I assume is the neighbor's grandson, walks inside to hug his "grandfather" and then me. Salim comes into the room, and he hugs him.

"This is the neighbor's son, Adam," he says.

"Nice to meet you, Adam," I say. I'm ashamed for assuming "grandfather." I hope my surprise doesn't show on my face.

Salim's mother places a large terra-cotta platter of couscous on the short round table. Salim pours glasses of Coke for the neighbor and Adam, Sprite for himself and me. His mother returns to the table, pouring the stewed chicken, pumpkin, onions, potatoes, and carrots on top of the yellow grains. There is a small bowl of broth to spoon over the dish as well as a carton of buttermilk to drink with it. She pours herself a glass of buttermilk. Salim gives us each a spoon, which we'll use to eat from the platter. "Yes," he says as we begin, spoon after spoon. I notice his mom is using her hands, making the couscous and broth and vegetables into small balls and eating them. Salim points to her. "This is how we used to eat couscous," he says.

The couscous is superb: hearty yet subtly flavored, nuanced, well seasoned, every food group well represented. The few times I'd had couscous in the United States didn't compare to this in the least.

There were moments when I could hear only our spoons tapping the platter or our teeth.

"Good?" Salim asks. I smile. He puts his spoon down, walks into the kitchen, and brings out a small plate of two roasted duck legs. "I don't like couscous that much," Salim says. "It doesn't work well in my stomach. My mom always makes these for me."

It is warm in that room. And the breeze, fragrant with good home-cooked food, mingles with alpine air. The front door is open as are the wood window shutters, the brown paint peeling from them.

There is the idea in Morocco about eating a meal together and how the act of sharing a meal connects the people around the table, makes them a quick family, links them. In this moment I feel this take root. The silver glow of the sun outside, on our spoons, on the plastic sofa coverings, on the silver chain of the neighbor, on Salim's mother's wedding band, on the metal tips of Adam's shoelaces, I see all of this. If that feeling of glow, both externally and within, if it can be seen, if it can show itself, it would look this way, a line of it arched and zigzagged through me, through us all. It is the thing that connects.

I eat around the chicken, filling my spoon with pumpkin, potato, zucchini, grains of couscous. Salim watches me then pulls a chunk of chicken from the bone and places it on my spoon. My pescatarian days are over. The spoon to my mouth is slow and once there, I chew and smile. I can't break the connection. I don't want to. But I know that refusing any part of it, rejecting any part of the main thing, the main meal, can and will break it.

When we finish, Salim brings a dish of fruit to the table. I take a pear, Salim an orange, the neighbor an apple, Adam a stem of purple grapes. Salim's mother prepares tea in the kitchen.

We are saying many things without words, in the silence. We are saying something about our beginning in this room and now. We are sated. We are filled with a newness, a knowledge of the existence of one another. We have been connected by a traditional North African meal. We are connected through kindness, out of kindness. Perhaps it is the need to be so or more specifically mine to feel. I'm so far from the places I recognize. But perhaps that's merely landscape, because I know friendship, its feeling, its beginning. I know what it's like to share. But this sharing is different; it's whole, generous, profoundly, purely welcoming.

Salim's mother pours tea in glasses. It foams at the top. We sip: once, twice before Salim puts on his shoes, and I follow, and we wave to the three left sipping.

"Thank you," I say to Salim's mother. I say the same to the neighbor. Adam hugs us before Salim and I leave.

Salim and I sit at the café where I bought the pastries earlier. He orders coffee and lights a cigarette. "Don't go to your class," he says, smoke curling from his mouth. "The day is so beautiful."

I want to stay. I want to talk. I want to continue building our friendship. I want to look at this light, this day's light. But I can't disappoint my students. But then I wonder if they'd be disappointed if I missed that day, if we had to wait to talk about the George Orwell essay I assigned, if we had to wait to discuss his take on colonialism, their colonialism, how we don't seem to decolonize, how we frequently think one way and act another.

"Thank you, Salim," I say before sipping that bitter espresso. I don't like coffee.

"It is nothing," he says.

"It's something," I say.

He tells me about his girlfriend visiting from Meknes this weekend and the apartment he's rented for them. "But I will pray first," he says. "Two nights together."

"May they be moonlit," I say. I laugh hearing myself.

"You are a poet."

"I am me." I look at my watch. If I get a taxi to campus now, I won't be late. I walk into the café and pay the waiter. I then sit back down.

"I'm going to watch *The Hurricane* tonight," Salim says.

"That's a good one. Denzel should have gotten the Oscar for it," I say.

Salim finishes his cigarette. "Coffee, Sunday?"

"Sure," I say, "You'll have a story to tell."

"I always have stories," he says before lighting another cigarette. I tell him I like his mother, the neighbor, and Adam. I ask him to tell his mother how grateful I am and how delicious her food is. "We'll have couscous again next week if you want," he says.

I tell him goodbye and run to the taxi. As I run he yells, "You are not in New York City. In Morocco, we do not run after taxis."

I'm one minute late to class. A quarter of the students are two minutes late.

We begin.

Top Ten Reasons I Love Morocco...
Roughly in the order I encountered them
by Zora O'Neill

1. **Zora, laundry lady of Tangier** — Never met her personally, but an influence on my whole life. More on this after the list.

2. **Pharmacist in Tangier** — She reached over the counter and squeezed my cheeks when I told her my name. More on this in a bit too.

3. **Goatherd in Chefchaouen** — On an ill-advised midday hike up the mountain behind Chefchaouen, with a travel partner who was still wondering why he'd come to Morocco at all instead of staying with a cute girl he'd met in Italy, we encountered a young man and his goats. In beautiful formal Arabic, the man told me he liked Belle and Sebastian (the cartoon, not the band) as well as singing to his goats. He demonstrated with a gorgeous classical song about the night and the desert and love. My travel partner and I walked back down that mountain with the silky music ringing in our ears, and he admitted it hadn't been a bad idea after all, coming to Morocco.

4. **Si Taoufec** — My Darija teacher in Fez, one of the most enthusiastic and dedicated teachers I've ever had. To my deep regret, by the time I got to his class, I was not only forty years old, with a nonabsorbent brain to match, but I'd also come from a year studying Arabic all across the Middle East and was simply confused and tired. My terrible Darija skills should in no way reflect this great teacher's talent.

5. **Houria of Rabat** — Houria befriended me on a train, and she happened to speak great Egyptian Arabic — the only dialect in which I can function reliably. Even in Egyptian, though, I missed the part where she explained that after we had dinner at her house, I'd be staying the night. Or maybe that was just a given? Dinner of cardoon tagine was dreamy and so was breakfast, and her parents were very kind to me even though I could barely communicate with them. Houria told me details about her own life that broke my heart but also made me admire her all the more.

6. **Aicha of Fez** — From this woman, who was the housekeeper for a place I stayed for a month, I got not just a recipe for *bsara*, a classic soup found all over Morocco, but the ingredients for it

as well. Aicha assembled a little bag of preportioned fava beans, green split peas, and little cloves of garlic. I think Aicha was eager to cook for me in part because her own daughter was a teenager who probably didn't get excited about anything her mom did for her.

7. **Masseuses in Fez** — They gave my friend and I a thorough hammam scrub and a solid massage. But where they really excelled was after, when we all sat in our bathrobes, drinking tea, and they shared their advice about men. "It's OK to wait till you're older to get married," they said. "Look for men who aren't babies, men who aren't scared of you. Children are important, but take care of yourself first." I'm already older and married, and I don't have children, but I share their advice here for others.

8. **Girl at the Jewish Cemetery** — A ten-year-old girl, a precocious tour guide if there ever was one, invited me up to her balcony to see the view over the Jewish cemetery in Fez. She took better photos than I did of the scenery, and made us pose for selfies. She served me mint tea, and then we played school: she was the teacher and I was the very bad student. Her mother showed me how to prepare cardoons.

9. **Hanae El Mouatamid** — I was walking through the Fez medina when a slim young woman with braces and glitter lipstick stopped me. "Do you have YouTube on your phone?" she asked. When I opened up the app, she went to her channel, and there she was in a slick video, singing a catchy pop song, looking gorgeous and glamorous and ten years older. When it was done, she pressed the subscribe button for me. All the while, her mother stood by, beaming proudly. They invited me to lunch at their house, but I was headed to another lunch date, and when they invited me again the next day, alas, I was already at the airport. Look her up on YouTube — she's lovely and she really can sing.

10. **Peaches** — "Moroccan peaches are the best in the world," Aicha the housekeeper declared. I've eaten peaches in a lot of

countries, and I concur. July in Fez may be hot, but it's worth it for the peaches.

* * *

I said I'd explain about Zora the laundry lady. She was a friend of my mother's when she and my father lived in Morocco before I was born, and I was named after her.

When I was a sulky preteen in 1980s America, I didn't like my name. It meant I couldn't buy personalized pencils at gift shops. My name had no *i* to dot with a heart. The part I did like was telling people how I got my name. At that age, I hadn't traveled anywhere or done anything particularly interesting, and my roots are Irish-English, so it was fun to conjure this place and my tenuous connection to it. Just pronouncing the syllables was incredibly thrilling: Tan-gier, Mo-roc-co.

When I was older, I came to like my name better, and I learned to tell the story a couple of different ways. When I was being sincere — infrequently; I was still young — I added that my mother's friend was an independent woman, a single mother who worked to support her family, which my mother admired. (I also used this strategy if I wanted to confound my listener's expectations about women in Morocco.) But if I was being glib, or if I wanted to puncture the exotic balloon I'd inflated by mentioning Tangier, I skipped the independence and said that I was named after a laundry lady.

My parents traveled a lot in Morocco, and I grew up hearing all their stories, eating cereal out of clay bowls they'd bought there, seeing my dad wear a dark-brown wool djellaba in the winter, hearing my mom call me with "Aji," an Arabic word she had picked up. So for all the exotic ring of Mo-roc-co, there was also a layer of ordinary domesticity to the word, a comfort in the name.

My first trip to Morocco was in 2000, when I was 28, the same age my mother had been when she was there. I saw many of the places my parents had told me about, walked in circles in the Fez medina, drank orange juice at every opportunity, and squabbled with my travel partner over how to spend our meager budget. I was also consumed with jealousy over that cute girl he'd met in Italy. I was still young — the Fez masseuses would say so, at least — so I was utterly consumed with this personal drama, and as a result, I let Morocco unfurl behind me like a backdrop. I met very few actual Moroccans.

From that first trip, however, I still recall two encounters with Moroccan people: the singing goatherd and the Tangier pharmacist. I said I would explain about her too.

Near the end of my trip, I went to a drugstore to buy some toothpaste, and the pharmacist asked me the usual questions: where was I from, how was I liking Morocco, and what was my name. When I told her I was American, I loved Morocco, and I was named after a woman from right here in Tangier, she reached over the counter and cupped my face in her hands and squealed, "Zweeeeeeeeyna!" (Lovely!)

"She's Moroccan," the pharmacist went on to say to her coworkers, turning my face to them, to show me off, and beaming at me in welcome. After nearly three decades of wrestling with my name and telling the story of it in various ways, I felt, in the touch of this woman's hands and her enthusiastic response, that it finally made sense for me to be who I was: Zora.

Or that's how I remember this encounter, anyway. I included the anecdote in a book that was published sixteen years later, a memoir about studying Arabic that included that first trip to Morocco — as well as several later trips, for which I was fortunately a bit less self-centered.

When I was writing that book, I went looking for the journal I remembered keeping on that first trip, but I found nothing. Just recently, though, in a box full of dreary business records, I came across a bright purple notebook, fat with pasted-in photos, bus tickets, and other ephemera.

When I was young, I didn't know how memory worked (or, really, how easily it failed). My journal was almost entirely about my emotional state, I suppose because I thought that was intangible and fleeting. As for the actual places we went, things we ate, and people we encountered, they were all so dramatic and striking that I assumed I would remember them forever. So I referred to them in an offhand way, with only the sketchiest detail.

The encounter with the Tangier pharmacist was one of these glossed-over moments, tacked at the end of a long lament about how stressful it was to share a hotel room with my travel partner. But, I was shocked to see, the journal had just enough detail to tell a very different story about the pharmacist from what I remembered.

Oddly, the incident had not come at the end of the trip, as I had recalled, but at the beginning. So meeting the woman was not a moment of synthesis, when all the strands of a story finally wove together. It was just a quick shopping trip in a place I'd just arrived, foolishly without any toothpaste.

Even more shocking, though, was that, according to my journal, the pharmacist had said not zweeeeeeeeyna, but ghareeeba.

Ghareeba means strange. It's a very different thing from zweyna, lovely.

It means the pharmacist must have seen an American woman with a Moroccan name and exclaimed about how odd it was, then showed off my oddness to her coworkers. The journal makes no mention of the pharmacist deeming me an honorary Moroccan. In short, the woman was probably pointing out what

I had also thought about my name, in my less grateful moments. It was a mismatch; it didn't fit; it was strange.

My memory twisted a story of one kind of confirmation — yup, a white American girl with a Moroccan name is just as weird as I thought — into another kind of confirmation, a far more lovely one. And I believed it enough to write it that way and have it published in a book that will sit on library shelves for a long time to come.

I don't know how it happened. I do know that I now love and appreciate my name and automatic connection it gave me to Morocco, and I believe I am an independent woman in part because of it. I suspect that, after carrying around this Moroccan name for so long, I wanted a moment in which I didn't have to tell any story about how I'd gotten it. And I guess I wanted it badly enough that I made it up. Or perhaps the memory changed simply to match my own impressions of the country. As I traveled more, Morocco eventually became, in my eyes, less strange and more lovely.

One thing that had puzzled me about the story of my name was how my mother had a Moroccan friend at all, when my mother spoke not much more Darija than "Aji," some rudimentary Spanish, and no French. "I guess Zora must have known a few English words?" she said when I asked her recently, but fifty years after the fact, she couldn't be sure.

After my repeat trips to Morocco, though, I eventually came to see how a friendship like my mother's could happen. When I went back on later trips — to work as a guidebook writer, to take Arabic classes, to escort friends around — I tried to make up for my youthful self-centeredness. I tried to appreciate the country for what it was, and not just how it measured up to my parents' stories or my childhood imaginings. I traveled by myself, and I tried to use whatever scraps of language I had. Which is how it has happened that, according to my Top Ten list, ninety percent of why I love Morocco is the people.

Of course I also love the great living craft traditions; the Fez medina free of cars, the scents of rosewater, orange blossom, and mint; the jewel-toned djellabas and the dazzling mosaics. But my experiences with Moroccans are my own, and I treasure them all the more because they can't be replicated (unless you want to study Darija with Si Taoufec at ALIF, which I really recommend).

And it's worth noting that, by the same list math, seventy percent of why I love Morocco is women. Travelers are almost always relegated to the public sphere: streets, cafes, museums, buses. But in Morocco, more than anywhere else I've visited, I've found myself welcomed warmly into private homes, almost always by exceptionally outgoing and engaging women. Even when that invitation was also a transaction — as it was with the enterprising girl at the Jewish cemetery — it was still an honest invitation to share in domestic life, a time to talk about daily things like fresh produce and homework.

And all those women managed to connect with me, regardless of language, whether it was the pharmacist cupping my face in her hands or Houria on the train altering her Arabic dialect so I could understand. Aicha, the Fez housekeeper, told me her whole life story — she, like my namesake, is a single mother — in a mix of simplest English and Arabic, and when she was finished the saga, we shared a long hug. After that, my mother's friendship with my namesake didn't seem puzzling at all.

It's easy to cast all these encounters in a warm glow, but then again, it would be dishonest to gloss over one common thread in many of them: so many of the stories Moroccan women have shared with me involve violence and tragedy, or, at best, disheartening social constraints and expectations. Abusive husbands, stillborn children, and Houria and I sleeping in the salon at her house, because she had no bedroom of her own; her parents hadn't built one in the new apartment because they'd expected her to be married already. I, a visitor, enjoyed the warmth, food, and intimacy of Moroccan domestic life — comforts that reminded me of my own parents and their stories and my earliest ideas of what Morocco was like. These women weathered all the rest.

My mother had no way to stay in touch with her Zora after she left Morocco. It was the late 1960s, and even if she had written a postcard, what language would she have written it in, and who would have read it to the woman? Zora is a distinctive name in America, but it's so common in Morocco that there's no way to trace her. The laundry lady who lived behind the Hotel Ourida in Tangier is likely lost to time.

The great benefit I enjoy now is all the ways I can stay in contact with the people I meet. Unfortunately I met Houria — who would be number one on the list if it were ordered by deepest connection and influence, instead of chronology — before smartphones were common, and international calls and messaging were expensive. She called me in New York once to ask if I'd found her a husband yet, but after a minute she ran out of credit. By the time I got back to Morocco, seven years had passed, and her number was no longer in service.

My more recent connections hold a bit better. I'm notified every time Hanae posts a new song on YouTube, and I can write and tell her she looks lovely and sounds lovelier. One day I hope to take her up on her lunch invitation. The older sister of the girl from the Jewish cemetery messages me sometimes too. And whenever I make bsara, I send a picture to Aicha in Fez.

Morocco Is

by Saeida Rouass

Morocco is the food you are forced to eat when you want fish fingers and chips. It is a tagine being cooked on the stove with fruit. It is round bread baked in the oven, a quarter of which is placed in front of you at the dinner table. It is being told you cannot leave the table until the bread is finished, and it is watching as the sun begins to set outside the kitchen window.

Morocco is the Arabic class you attend on Sundays at Regent's Park Mosque. It is squirming in your place as the teacher recites the alphabet over and over and verses from the Quran repeated until they are embedded into your memory even though you don't know what they mean. It is sitting in the classroom watching the clock tick on the wall and wondering how much time you will have to chase your friends through the mosque corridors and gardens.

Morocco is being taught how to pray when all you really want to do is play. It is an order to complete your ablutions and an order to line up behind your father as he recites the call to prayer. It is prostrating as he prostrates and trying to not laugh as from the corner of your eye you catch your sister doing a silly dance. It is knowing that God knows and sees everything.

Morocco is having people you don't know live with you. It is arriving home from school to be told that you need to move out of your bedroom and in with your sister because the two women sitting on the sofa looking quite stunned now live with you. It is hearing them tell their story to your mother as you try to watch *EastEnders*. It is hearing how they came to London with the Saudi family they worked for and fled the hotel and the abuse at the first opportunity. How they made their way to your uncle because they had heard about a Moroccan restaurant in Soho and how he had brought them to your mother for safe keeping. It is bumping into them on the street when you are older, them married with children and swooping you up in a hug and crying at the sight of you.

Morocco is a destination of childhood. It is the place you make your way to on the first day of summer school holidays. It is leaving the school gates and running home to find your belongings already packed and in the car ready for the dawn journey.

Morocco is driving through Europe, sometimes alone and sometimes in a convoy with others all making their way to Tangier. It is stopping at roadside service stations in France to use the bathrooms and begging your father for an espresso.

It is playing a game of spotting other Moroccans on the same journey, heading towards the same destination. It is looking at the license plates of their cars and guessing which European country they have come from. It is breaking down in Spain and waiting for a tow truck and getting a fever and being treated by the Red Cross on the side of the road. It is eating tuna from a can and looking out of the window at a never-ending road.

Morocco is Larache and summers spent jumping on boats to be taken over to the beach. It is sitting on the beach all day eating nothing but a doughnut. It is being followed, whistled at, touched, and threatened. It is cocooning yourself within the protective bubble of other Moroccans from Europe and spending days and evenings with friends from London whom you only ever see in Morocco. It is traveling to the mountains to visit your grandfather and him calling you his liver, even though he forgets your name. It is endless kisses from adults who are cousins and uncles and great-uncles and aunts and taken to the hammam and scrubbed until you're raw and made to sit in the steam until you almost pass out.

Morocco is a distant a part of you that you want to disown. It is a legacy you inherited. It is a thing to be downplayed and described as belonging to your parents as you begin to navigate adulthood. It is an identity that others find a novelty. It is a joke, and you are the punch line. It is Arabian nights and forced marriages. It is Jimi Hendrix and the hippie trail. It is exotic and oppressive to women. It is what your new friends at university perceive it to be, based on hundreds of years of oriental imagery and storytelling.

Morocco is a forgotten thing. It is a thing that others look for in you that you don't deny or promote. It is the thing that makes you not British. It is a source of confusion and a cause to explain your existence. It is what makes you a stranger at home and at home in a strange place. It is what makes you a foreigner when in Morocco and an immigrant in England. Morocco is you in the eyes of others.

Morocco is more than Larache. It is trips to Essaouira and Gnawa music late into the night. It is a snake charmer in

Marrakesh and Alpha Blondy in Fez. It is camel trips into the Sahara and an ancient travel route from Timbuktu to Tangier. It is bargaining in the market while knowing you are being ripped off. It is letting you think you know it, when really you know nothing.

Morocco is rediscovered. It is summers showing the place off to friends and discovering it anew. It is a tourist trap that makes you cool. It is astonishment on the faces of the visitors you induct. It is hair-raising taxi rides to the Blue Pearl that you shrug off as part of its charm. It is a source of cultural pride.

Morocco is Larache. It is old cameras sold on sidewalks and families promenading. It is women shelling prawns in factories and young men selling gadgets to make a living. It is a people not broken. It is late nights with a blind great-uncle and his deaf wife and a history lost in their passing. It is a heritage discovered and its wisdom learnt.

Morocco is common ground. It is a woman in Malaysia bonding with you because you are Moroccan. It is a man in Oman calling you sister. It is a taxi driver in Cairo calling his daughter Saeida. It is a landlady in Tunisia serving you tea that you know and a bank clerk in Ethiopia reminding you that you are both African. It is children in Jordan laughing at your Arabic dialect and unlikely friendships born from shared identities.

Morocco is a story. It is the books written by Europeans. It is an inspiration for painters, authors, and oddballs. It is stories untold and voices not heard. It is a woman who knows herself even when others don't or when they choose to misrepresent her.

Morocco is rediscovered. It is not a postcard. It is so much more. It is its complexities and contradictions. It is a look that completes your sentence. It is a conversation loaded with hidden meaning. It is an instinct discovered and a knowledge tapped. It is solidarity with strangers and shared successes.

Morocco is its history. It is Marrakesh in 1906. It is a Sufi brotherhood that eats only fruit. It is resistance to colonial powers. It is a battle cry and the hand that wipes your tears when you fail.

Morocco is home. It is a smell that greets you on arrival and nourishes your soul. It is familiar alleyways and a humor learnt over time. It is arguments in taxis that end in handshakes. It is an unspoken understanding.

Morocco

is

my

teacher.

About the Authors

Zakariaa Aitouraies is one of the youngest Moroccan writers to author a book in English. He was born in 1997 in a small town seventy kilometers (about forty miles) southeast of Casablanca. After graduating high school, he went on to study English at Hassan II university. At the age of twenty-two, after getting his BA, he self-published his first book, *When the Night Sleeps: A Collection of Short Stories and Poems*. He is currently working on publishing his second book and pursuing a Masters' degree. You can follow Zackariaa on Instagram @zack.aitouraies or find out more about him on his website, www.zakariaaaitouraies.com.

Hazim Azghari Born and raised in Northwest Africa, Hazim has spent a lot of time around the Mediterranean while growing up. Over time, his bookish interests and love for the landscape have converged to focus on the historical relationship between humans and nature. An environmentalist by training, he has worked in environmental NGOs for a few years and also taught environmental subjects at an undergraduate level, both with a focus on climate change adaptation, plastic pollution, and the history of environmentalism.

Dina Benbrahim is an Arab multidisciplinary creative who uses a feminist lens to focus on illuminating the power in human beings to be transformative forces in society. Her current research investigates design for civic action and social justice for marginalized communities to collectively reimagine equitable futures. She is now an Assistant Professor in Design at University at Buffalo, State University of New York, motivated to activate greatness in everyone she encounters. You can find out more about her work at dinabenbrahim.com and @dina.benbrahim on Instagram.

Suzanna Clarke moved to Morocco in 2011. Since then, she has lived in the Fez Medina with her husband, novelist Sandy McCutcheon, and their two children. Originally from New Zealand and Australia, she has been a photographer, journalist, and the Arts Editor of a large Australian newspaper. Her bestselling book, *A House in Fez: Building a Life in the Ancient Heart of Morocco*, was published in the US, UK, Australia, New Zealand, Poland, and Korea. Suzanna has restored several historic properties and owns accommodation businesses in Morocco and France. In 2015, she started the Fez Medina Children's Library with two friends, which continues to inspire local children.

Eirlys Davies has lived in Morocco since 1982 and taught first at Sidi Mohammed Ben Abdellah University in Fez before moving to teach at King Fahd School of Translation in Tangier.

Richard Hamilton co-authored the *Time Out Guide to Marrakech* while living in Morocco in 2006 and 2007. His best-known works include: *The Last Storytellers: Tales from the Heart of Morocco* (IB Tauris, 2011) and *Tangier: From the Romans to the Rolling Stones* (Bloomsbury in 2019). Richard has been a BBC journalist since 1995, and their correspondent in Morocco, South Africa and Madagascar. He was also the Africa Editor for BBC World Service radio and is now a general international news reporter. Before joining the BBC, he worked as a solicitor, night porter, ski guide and dish-washer.

Myronn Hardy is the author of, most recently, *Radioactive Starlings*, published by Princeton University Press (2017). His poems have appeared in *The New York Times Magazine*, *The Baffler*, *Virginia Quarterly Review*, *Belleville Park Pages* (Paris), and elsewhere. He lived in Morocco for almost a decade. He teaches at Bates College.

Lynn Houmdi is known in Essaouira as "Madame Cimitière" for her work on local history and rehabilitation of the cemeteries of the Christian, Jewish, and Muslim faiths. She is a genuine expert on all things Swiri (Essaouiran), having lived in the bohemian fishing town on Morocco's Atlantic Coast for a number of years. In 2018, she conducted an ethnographic study of the town's unemployed graduates for her master's degree in Islamic and Middle Eastern Studies, for which she received a prize from the University of Edinburgh. Lynn divides her time with her Swiri husband and their son between Essaouira and Edinburgh, Scotland. As well as writing and consulting for various clients with an interest in Morocco, she supports nonprofits and small businesses to grow and communicate with purpose. You can find more writing by Lynn on her blog, maroc-o-phile.com or follow her on Twitter (@maroc_o_phile).

Amina Lahbabi is a Communication for Development specialist. She has worked on large international projects in many countries in the MENA region and Europe with the United Nations and the European Commission with UNESCO. Amina is a Fulbright Scholar. She holds an M.A. in advertising at Michigan State University in addition to her M.A. in Translation at King Fahd School of Translation (Arabic, English, French, and Spanish). She supports many sustainable initiatives around Morocco, a country she loves to photograph whenever she has a moment. After some time living in the US and France, she now lives in Tangier, where she was born and raised.

Gerald Loftus, a retired American diplomat living in Brussels, was director of the Tangier American Legation Institute for Moroccan Studies (TALIM) from 2010 to 2014. He is the author of *Lions at the Legation & Other Tales: Two Centuries of American Diplomatic Life in Tangier*.

Alice Morrison is an adventurer and an explorer. She has travelled to the furthest places on earth and walk through its toughest habitats. In 2016-17 she filmed the BBC2 documentary series, *From Morocco to Timbuktu: An Arabian Adventure*. Her quest was an epic journey along the ancient salt roads, over the snow-covered Atlas Mountains and across the Saharan sands. Alice's latest book, *Adventures in Morocco* (Simon & Schuster, 2019), is the story of her life in Morocco so far which is sometimes hard, sometimes hilarious and always interesting. Discover more on her website: www.alicemorrison.co.uk.

Amanda Mouttaki is an American who has lived in Marrakesh since 2012 with her husband and three children. She runs the website www.MarocMama.com and Marrakech Food Tours, both of which aim to help visitors bridge the gap between their home and Morocco

Zora O'Neill is the author of *All Strangers Are Kin: Adventures in Arabic and the Arab World*, which was awarded the Lowell Thomas Award for Best Travel Book of 2016 by the Society of American Travel Writers. She was raised in New Mexico and has lived in Astoria, New York, since 1998. She writes about travel in the broadest sense, about anyone who makes their way around the globe. Her writing on refugees in Greece has appeared everywhere from *USA Today* to *Parnassus: Poetry in Review*. She grew up in New Mexico, where the terrain is not so different from Morocco's, and now lives in New York City, coincidentally in a neighborhood with a lot of Moroccans. Read more at zoraoneill.com.

Lucas Peters is an award-winning writer, photographer and Morocco expert. He is the author and principal photographer of the Moon Country Guidebook for Morocco and Marrakesh and Beyond, as well as hundreds of other articles, photos and videos for magazines and websites around the world. In addition, he curates and edits the award-winning Morocco travel blog for Journey Beyond Travel, where he is now the Managing Director. He lives in Tangier with his wife and kids. Connect with Lucas anywhere on social media or through his website: www.lucasmpeters.com.

Saeida Rouass is of Moroccan heritage, born and raised in London. She spent ten years working internationally as a trainer and project manager for various charities and NGOs. She currently works within international development and security with a focus on the Middle East & North Africa, and Morocco in particular. She is the author of *Eighteen Days of Spring in Winter* (Impress Books, 2015) and *Assembly of the Dead* (Impress Books, 2017). She is currently working on *Library of Untruths*, set in 1912 Fez, when Morocco became a French Protectorate, as well as the sequel to *Assembly of the Dead*.

Tahir Shah is a prolific best-selling author and film-maker. His thirty-year career has produced more than forty highly acclaimed works of fiction and non-fiction, as well as numerous documentaries and screenplays, and a massive body of journalism, scholarly articles, and photography. Tahir has spent his professional life searching for the hidden underbelly of lands through which he travels. In doing so he often uncovers layers of life that most other writers hardly even realize exist. With a world-wide following, Tahir's work has been translated into more than thirty languages, in hundreds of editions. His documentaries have been screened on National Geographic TV, The History Channel, Channel 4, and in cinemas the world over.

www.ingramcontent.com/pod-product-compliance
Lightning Source LLC
LaVergne TN
LVHW042348250625
814744LV00006B/156